Leasing for Shopping Center
Non-Leasing Professionals

LEASING FOR SHOPPING CENTER NON-LEASING PROFESSIONALS

International Council of Shopping Centers
New York

About the International Council of Shopping Centers

The International Council of Shopping Centers (ICSC) is the trade association of the shopping center industry. Serving the shopping center industry since 1957, ICSC is a non-for-profit organization with more than 67,000 members in 100 countries worldwide. ICSC members include shopping center

- owners
- developers
- managers
- marketing specialists
- leasing agents
- retailers
- researchers
- attorneys

- architects
- contractors
- consultants
- investors
- lenders and brokers
- academics
- public officials

ICSC holds more than 200 meetings a year and provides a wide array of services and products for shopping center professionals, including publications and research data.

For more information about ICSC, please contact:
International Council of Shopping Centers
1221 Avenue of the Americas
New York, NY 10020-1099
Telephone (646) 728-3800
info@icsc.org
Fax: (732) 694-1755
www.icsc.org

Companies, professional groups, clubs and other organizations may qualify for special terms when ordering quantities of more than 20 of this title.

Published by
International Council of Shopping Centers
Publications Department
1221 Avenue of the Americas
New York, NY 10020-1099
www.icsc.org

International Standard Book Numbers 1-58268-071-x
978-1-58268-071-2

ICSC Catalog Number: 293

Contents

3. Prospecting for Tenants   33
Heather L. Herring

4. The Art of the Deal   45
Steven W. Toppel, CLS

5. The Lease and Its Administration   57
John L. Gerdes, SCSM, CLS, CPM

About This Book

As a shopping center professional, you have unique information needs about leasing. For example, you may need to know how to prospect for tenants, the effects of the market on the clauses of a lease and how to effectively use a pro forma, among other topics.

Leasing for Shopping Center Non-Leasing Professionals provides you with practical information on leasing terms and principles used in the shopping center industry. Each chapter is derived from a presentation of the curriculum of ICSC's Leasing for Non-Leasing educational seminar and has been contributed by a shopping center professional with leasing expertise. The contributors have clarified explanations of leasing terms and principles with examples and charts specific to shopping centers within their spheres of experience.

Subjects covered in *Leasing for Shopping Center Non-Leasing Professionals* include the following:

- History and evolution of shopping center leasing
- Pro formas and leasing strategy
- Prospecting for tenants
- Essential lease clauses
- Retailer's perspective on leasing
- Specialty leasing strategies
- Tenant coordination
- Negotiating

A useful glossary and index are also included for reader convenience.

Acknowledgments

The International Council of Shopping Centers gratefully acknowledges the following shopping center professionals who contributed to this book.

Robert E. Young, Jr.
Managing Director
The Weitzman Group
Dallas, Texas

John N. Desco, SCSM, SCLS
Senior Vice President,
   Asset Management
Coyote Management, L.P.
Addison, Texas

Heather L. Herring
Corporate Communications and
   Marketing Director
The MGHerring Group, Inc.
Dallas, Texas

Steven W. Toppel, CLS
Group Vice President of Leasing
General Growth Properties, Inc.
Irving, Texas

John L. Gerdes, SCSM, CLS, CPM
Vice President, Asset Management
L & B Realty Advisors, LLP
Dallas, Texas

Craig B. Sorrels
Principle
CSWG, Inc.
Dallas, Texas

Camilla L. Basse
Prime Retail
San Marcos, Texas

Karen M. Scott, SCMD
Director of Tenant Coordination
Urban Related Management
New York City, New York

Steve Weingarten
Senior Vice President
Weingarten Realty Investors
Houston, Texas

Ian D. Pierce
Director of Corporate Communications
The Weitzman Group/Cencor
   Realty Services
Dallas, Texas

Leasing for Shopping Center Non-Leasing Professionals

1

The Universe of Leasing

Robert E. Young, Jr., and Ian D. Pierce

Retail real estate encompasses a diverse group of brokers, developers, investors, retailers, property managers and others, who all understand that leasing is the heart of successful retail projects.

These people know that the right retail concepts are the key to retail success, and that even the best retailers can do better when they have a leasing agent who understands co-tenancy and tenant-mix issues.

Good leasing agents also understand what retailers are all about. These agents help create centers that offer a mix of retailers that complement one another.

What are our favorite places to shop? Those places that have a collection of retailers with that perfect balance between what we need and what we want. The kind of place where people find things they just have to have, even if they never knew that these things existed before.

People get that kind of shopping environment thanks to a retail leasing agent. Those places don't happen by accident—they happen because of professionals who understand the art and science of retail leasing.

Leasing agents are on the frontlines with retailers. They understand what retailers want and need. They convey retailers' requirements to the architects, to the developers and to the marketing people.

Basically, a center can be beautiful, with all the bells and whistles, but if it doesn't work for retailers in terms of location and layout, then it is going to fail.

History and Evolution of Leasing

To understand leasing, consider the history and evolution of leasing. Case studies are plentiful, such as two Dallas malls that followed very different paths. Although both of these centers are in Dallas, their story is repeated across the country and can be found in many markets.

One of the centers is Big Town, Dallas's first mall and the first air-conditioned shopping center in the Southwest. Big Town opened in 1959 to great fanfare. The *Dallas Morning News* dedicated a 24-page section to the opening. People came from miles around to be a part of history. Today the mall itself is gone: in late 2006, bulldozers removed the last traces of Big Town from the landscape.

What happened? Or rather, what didn't happen? Big Town did not change with the times. Big Town in 1989 or 1999 hadn't changed from 1959, although it may have looked a little tired, and the merchants were less successful than at the start. The mall tried to hang on after its anchors pulled out, one by one—but the writing was on the wall.

Six years after Big Town made news, NorthPark opened in 1965. The mall started with three department stores, including Neiman Marcus at one end and JCPenney at the other. Retail went through major changes in the 40 years after NorthPark opened. But the mall continued to thrive. Why?

NorthPark's leasing agents paid attention to the customers that NorthPark attracted. They noticed that the Neiman's store pulled in affluent shoppers. They started to transform much of the mall into a collection of upper-end retailers. The area around NorthPark continued to become more affluent, but there were middle-income customers in the area, too. NorthPark's leasing agents worked hard to find the right mix to make all those different customers feel welcome.

The mall continued to upgrade. Each time a retailer went out, the agents worked hard to find a better one to replace it. The mall's ownership and management, meanwhile, worked just as hard to keep the mall looking great.

The team was successful. Recently, NorthPark completed an expansion program that nearly doubled the mall's size to two million square feet. North Park is one example of what dedicated, professional leasing agents, working with a proactive ownership and management team, can do for a center.

Changing Trends

The retail market continues to change. Leasing agents need to understand those changes so they can stay one step ahead.

To appreciate the current universe of leasing, it helps to know its past.

SHOPPING CENTERS SINCE 1960

Many people see the 1960s as the true start of the modern shopping center environment. In the 1960s, suburban centers started to lure retailers from downtowns. These centers catered to the suburban growth that resulted in part from the birth of the interstate highway system. Almost overnight, people could live miles from their work due to the access provided by the superhighways. As new rooftops sprang up, retail followed.

In the 1970s, the enclosed mall went through one of its biggest growth periods ever. The first enclosed malls came into being in the late 1950s, then saw growth in the 1960s. As those malls found great success, more and more were built in the 1970s. Many of these took advantage of the strong regional locations and access created by new highways.

In the 1980s, community centers became king as grocers expanded rapidly for a growing population.

In the 1990s, the birth of category killers led to a power center boom. During this period, power centers opened at regional locations, often around malls. It was then that huge 300,000- to 600,000-square-foot centers came to be the norm, rather than the exception.

In the 2000s, lifestyle and mixed-use centers are thriving as consumers seek a "sense of place." It is somewhat ironic that the modern retail story began with an exodus of retailers from central cities and now, more than 40 years later, the most current centers are trying to re-create that sense of a downtown shopping district. In fact, suburban cities across the country are creating "town squares"— brand-new town centers with a mix of retail, residential, office, service and municipal uses. These town squares typically are designed to be pedestrian-friendly locations that mimic old-time downtowns.

CHANGING ANCHORS

Market drivers propelled all these changes—the retailers with the force to justify a shopping center. These drivers also saw changes during the same 40-year period.

In the 1960s, discounters were the big drivers. In Dallas-Fort Worth, Woolco and Fed-Mart were two of the biggest, and neither of them is around today. The 1960s also saw the birth of the boutique store.

In the 1970s, department stores were the big drivers. This coincided with the growth of the regional mall concepts. In Dallas-Forth Worth, the big guns were Titche's, Sanger-Harris, JCPenney and Montgomery Ward. Only JCPenney's is still around.

Titchés became Joske's became Dillard's. Sanger-Harris became Foley's became Macy's. With each name change, these department stores went from a local force to a regional one and, finally, to a national one. The same consolidation has occurred in almost every retail category.

In the 1980s, the traditional grocery store became the king of market drivers. During this decade, grocers enlarged their stores with more categories than ever. The new grocery superstore absorbed the florist, the card shop, the camera shop, the deli, the bakery and other specialties.

This had a huge impact on leasing plans. Leasing agents in the 1980s saw that their anchor tenants suddenly absorbed a large range of targeted retail uses, so they adapted. Community centers saw the grocery stores get bigger and the in-line spaces get smaller. That completely changed the leasing strategy for this category of center.

Today, other categories of shopping centers are on the cusp of this kind of change. The traditional enclosed mall, for example, is changing. The mall's traditional anchor—the department store—isn't necessarily the driver it used to be, as active department store anchors in each market are looking toward open-air formats as a way to revitalize themselves.

"Category killers" were the boom driver in the 1990s. Category killers are large-format retailers whose focus is very narrow but whose selection is very deep. Category killers are the opposite of the department store or general merchandise retailer. Category killers started with Toys "Я" Us and took off from there.

These types of retailers today have at least two major competitors in each category. For every Barnes & Noble, there is a Borders. For each Bed Bath & Beyond, there is a Linens 'n Things.

These concepts survived even though their competitors failed. It seems that every time a hot new retail concept comes along, a growth period follows when a lot of concepts compete for the same dollar. Often, eventually, only two main competitors are left standing.

The 2000s are seeing growth at two ends of the spectrum. At one end is the lifestyle retailer category. Lifestyle retailers are designed to meet the wants and needs of a casual lifestyle. To understand the lifestyle center, put together a group like Z Gallerie, Chico's, Williams-Sonoma, Talbots, Gap, White House/Black Market and Cheesecake Factory.

At the other end of the spectrum—the end where every penny counts—is perhaps this decade's most important anchor, Wal-Mart Supercenter. These supercenters almost overnight became the leading grocer in some of the largest markets. They shook up the traditional grocery market. Even in markets where traditional grocers still lead, those traditional grocers are basing their plans on Wal-Mart. Leading Texas grocer H-E-B, for example, is active with a 150,000- to 170,000-square-foot concept called H-E-B Plus!, a direct competitor with Wal-Mart.

Wal-Mart is the reason that the traditional grocery store is no longer the retail king it used to be. In Dallas-Fort Worth and markets across the country, grocery stores are closing and, in some cases, exiting certain competitive markets entirely.

Today's leasing agents have to understand Wal-Mart Supercenter. They have to understand what type of customer Wal-Mart attracts, what retailers compete with Wal-Mart and what retailers are complementary to Wal-Mart, because Wal-Mart is figuring out a way to attract those leasing agents' customers.

OTHER CHANGES

What else has happened since 1960? The biggest change is that retail has gone from the central cities and the neighborhoods to regional retail districts. It's not unusual for markets to have two or three or four million square feet at one intersection.

The other big change is the size of retailers. Grocery stores are a textbook example of how store sizes change. For years, grocery stores were around 30,000 to 40,000 square feet. Then they added categories and grew to today's average of 75,000 square feet. The success of Wal-Mart is causing grocers to go to 170,000-square-foot stores.

What does that mean to community centers typically anchored by a grocery store? In the 1960s, when the grocery store was small, the in-line space was a lot larger. Let's take a 100,000-square-foot center. In 1960, that center had a 30,000- to 40,000-square-foot grocery store as its anchor. The in-line space was occupied by dress shops, a florist, a card shop, a deli and so on. Now the grocery store is 80,000 square feet or more, and the florist and the deli and the card shop are inside the grocery store.

What this did was turn the in-line space into neighborhood-oriented retail. The limited in-line space in today's community center is devoted to tax offices, medical space and perhaps a Starbucks. In other words, the community center has become a center that serves the neighborhood's day-to-day needs. When people want soft goods, they go to the regional retail district, where they can find almost every store they can imagine.

The Art of Retail Leasing

As markets go through these changes, leasing agents need to stay one step ahead because major change is going on every day. The basics of leasing, however, have stayed the same.

BASIC PRINCIPLES

These basic principles are market knowledge, professionalism and customer service. Furthermore, customer service in the real estate industry entails more than the usual nine-to-five hours and five-day work week. Herb Weitzman, former ICSC trustee and chairman, stresses the importance of customer service as well as making the most of opportunities.

One of his most successful business relationships began on a Sunday when he got a call from real estate executives from the discount chain Fed-Mart who wanted to see properties that day. Herb, of course, met with them and not only leased a center, but began a relationship built on his professionalism and service. Years later, even after the chain ceased to exist, Herb was able to continue to do business with the people in that company. He also purchased the properties and used the market knowledge developed in this relationship to place anchor tenants such as Kroger and Oshman's Sporting Goods in spots where Fed-Mart had been.

WHAT HAS STAYED THE SAME?

Following are some important basics:

- Know the market.
- Be prepared to work when it is convenient for the client.
- Real estate is not a transaction business, it is a relationship business.

Finally, good real estate is good real estate. The locations that worked for Fed-Mart in the 1960s later worked for Marshalls in the 1980s. Now, one of those locations is a brand-new Lowe's store. That's what a good leasing agent understands. No matter how many changes there are in retailers and centers, there is always a user for good real estate.

There are other basics that are as important today as they were 40 years ago. The leasing agent must know the market, but also:

- The leasing agent must know the product.
- The prospect should get to the property.

- The leasing agent should be able to talk up the location in terms of sales, not rents.

Retailers don't pay $50 per square foot rents because they're looking for the highest rents in the market. They pay them because they're looking for the highest sales in the market. Centers with killer locations, tenant mixes and traffic can get high rents because they can generate high sales.

WHAT HAS CHANGED?

If these basics have stayed the same, then what has changed?

Retailers are more sophisticated today. They know how to negotiate for every advantage they can get, so the leasing agent has to understand lease restrictions. He or she has to understand what these restrictions mean to the leasing program and to the center's co-tenancy. They also need to understand which restrictions are negotiable and which are set in stone.

Today's leasing agents also have to understand co-tenancy like never before. At the start of the mall business, a shopper would find similar concepts at opposite ends of the mall. The leasing agents kept, for example, the high-end dress shops away from one another.

Now when shoppers go to the mall, those similar concepts are grouped together. Retailers and leasing agents understand that a collection of retailers in the same category can work together as a magnet to draw traffic much more effectively than a single retailer in that category.

That's why in many markets, there is a home furnishings center next to IKEA. You would think that furniture retailers would want to stay out of the shadow of this 350,000-square-foot gorilla of a furniture store. Instead, they know that IKEA will draw furniture shoppers like bees to honey. And they want to locate where those shoppers are.

One of the biggest changes for leasing agents can be seen in retailers' expectations. In the 1980s, retailers had large real estate departments that dealt with local brokers. Now, if a retailer does have a real estate department, it's smaller, and it looks to the leasing agent to augment the department. Today, leasing agents supply demographics, mapping, sales forecasts, sales trends, competitor and complementary use analysis and site-by-site analysis. This requires brokerage firms to invest a lot of money in research. At many firms, research is one of its biggest budget items.

Technology is another big change. Today, leasing agents have to understand and communicate through:

- e-mail
- e-marketing
- Web sites and
- Mapping software

Modern Leasing Team Theory

THE LEASING REP

One of the biggest changes for leasing agents can be seen in the area of specialization. The earliest leasing agents were general brokers, handling leasing, sales, ranch properties, retail properties, perhaps even a little residential. Now specialization is the norm, not the exception.

While there are changes yet to come, one trait about leasing agents was true at the beginning and will remain true: a leasing agent is able to command a room, to control a process and to sell, sell, sell. The leasing agent is supported by many people and functions.

RESEARCH

A good team usually includes the research department, since research can make a cold call work. To cold-call Retailer A, the leasing agent will need to identify Retailer A's best locations. Then the agent's research department can help determine the parameters of those locations, including demographics: incomes, number of households, families with kids, and so on. Then the agent can locate competing uses and complementary uses in the trade area, among other factors.

Then the agent might work with the research department to uncover similar trade areas throughout the submarkets where Retailer A has no presence.

So on the cold call, the agent doesn't just ask Retailer A for his business. The leasing agent comes armed with information that benefits Retailer A. The agent can show Retailer A how they can be partners by showing an understanding of the retailer's business and what the retailer needs to succeed.

MARKETING

Marketing support is another key member of the leasing team. Whether it's as simple as a flier or as advanced as a complete Web site, marketing gets the word out about a center.

An example of how marketing works with leasing comes from The Triangle, a project that is being developed with 120,000-square-foot small-tenant specialty space in central Austin.

The leasing program is creating a collection of Austin-centric retailers, meaning retailers that are a little funky, a little unusual. The problem was that the market saw The Triangle as a standard retail center. The leasing agents couldn't get much interest from their targeted retailers. The marketing team talked to the developer and leasing agent and saw a way to solve the problem.

Marketing pitched the story to the local business journal, pointing out how unusual it was for a brand-new center to go after local tenants only. The story ended up running on the front page of the business journal. The headline was: "TRIANGLE ZEROES IN ON UNIQUE RETAILERS." The result? The leasing agents started getting calls from the very retailers that hadn't shown much interest before. The marketing team understood the problem and positioned the center to overcome it.

PROPERTY MANAGEMENT

The last key member of the leasing team is property management (although there are other team members). Basically, property management makes a center look good and keeps the tenants happy. Good management understands that its task is to add value to real estate. Successful management considers the needs of three elements: the shopper, the tenant and the owner.

Pro Formas and Leasing Strategy

Leasing agents also need to understand the concept of the pro forma and how it shapes leasing strategies and vice versa.

A pro forma is an estimate or a budget focused on the end result. The pro forma is based on investment objectives that are balanced with what the market will bear. The owner may say he needs a 15-percent return on investment. The leasing agent can create a pro forma—a budget—that delivers that return, and shows how it is achievable based on what the market will allow.

The pro forma has to consider market dynamics and cost—land, construction, capital improvements, fees. Those costs are measured against expectations of revenue—that is, what rents can the center achieve, and for how long?

A pro forma cannot exist in a bubble. It has to take market factors into account. For example, if a landlord creates a pro forma that does not allow for adequate tenant improvement (TI), but the market is such that the retail tenant community demands big TI, the result is that the pro forma is unrealistic. It can't be achieved given market dynamics.

This leaves the retail leasing strategy in a conundrum. The tenants won't sign leases without TI, and the pro forma won't be achieved if TI is given. Clearly, a pro forma cannot be constructed from an isolationist's perspective. It has to take into account what is really happening—and what is likely to happen—in the market. Otherwise, the pro forma ends up having no flexibility, especially if the market does a downturn. That kind of pro forma completely handcuffs the leasing strategy. Leases become almost impossible to execute because you can't give retailers the things that are necessary to get the deals done at that point in time.

The best pro formas are created when the leasing team and the developer work hand in hand. The leasing team is out there in the market. It knows the market realities. It can help avoid problems with the pro forma by being a part of the process. The leasing team can analyze the relationship between the retailers' plans and the developer's plans.

Developers' Goals Versus Retailers' Goals

The needs of the retailer and the leasing goals of the developer should absolutely be in alignment more times than not—or they wouldn't be in business. If, for example, a developer simply develops properties without any sense of what tenants need and want and of how tenants thrive, then that developer won't be developing for too long.

More than ever before, it seems developers are more in tune with what retailers need. Each time a new project is built, it reflects another level of sensitivity to the retailer's end game.

Development succeeds because it is done from a retailer's standpoint, so there is a co-dependency. Both of these key parties have to work together. The leasing agent understands where the parties can work together and where they can diverge. Where developers and retailers most often diverge is on the issue of profitability:

- The landlord wants maximum retail income.
- The tenant wants the most manageable occupancy costs to generate higher net revenue.

THE COMPROMISE IS PERCENTAGE RENT

What compromise has evolved to bridge this convergence—this gap between the developer's and the retailer's goals? The simple answer is: percentage rent.

Percentage rent is the developer's way of working with a retailer to keep its occupancy cost at a certain level as long as its sales are at a certain level. But if the developer's project is so outstanding that the retailer does more business than expected, the developer then shares in that success.

Percentage rent is paid only after a retailer exceeds an established sales breakpoint. On sales in excess of that breakpoint, the retailer pays the developer a percentage of sales. Since percentage rent is a function of sales, it is in the interest of the developer to do everything to make the retailer as successful as possible.

The developer tells the retailer, "I get more rent if you're successful." The retailer tells the developer, "I'll pay more rent if I'm successful."

Percentage rent creates reliance between the landlord and the retailer. It is a perfect example of a win-win situation.

The Marketplace—Its Role in Retail Leasing

Retail doesn't exist in a bubble. More than many other industries, retail is affected by economic conditions, both good and bad.

This effect goes back to the pro forma and the issue of the relationship between the developer and the retailer—particularly, those market forces that on the surface have no direct relationship to retail sales or shopping centers can actually have a huge impact.

These forces include but are not limited to population growth, housing growth—or the lack thereof—interest rates, global concerns, environmental issues, government issues such as taxation, economic issues and so on. Each one of these factors, on its own, doesn't make the difference in whether a consumer buys a pair of shoes or not, but at the end of the day, market conditions work together to affect the amount of disposable income available to buy goods or services.

POSITIVE AND NEGATIVE ECONOMIC CONDITIONS

One example can be seen in the impact of $3-a-gallon-plus gasoline in the marketplace. What we expect to be true is not necessarily true. For example, GM released a new line of giant SUVs just as gas hit $3 a gallon. People expected the sales of SUVs to drop. Instead, sales went up significantly because many consumers do not base decisions on prices. They base their decisions on preferences.

But $3-a-gallon gas has had a negative impact on retailers at the lower end. Wal-Mart's same-store sales have been below target, because Wal-Mart's core customer is affected a lot more by $3-a-gallon gas than, say, the Whole Foods customer.

Market forces can change shopping habits. Given high gas prices, some consumers would rather drive to a big retail district than drive all over town to visit stores. As a result, concentrations of regional retail can benefit as people try to conserve gas. People can drive to one shopping district and find just about every major retailer possible.

DEVELOPMENT AND ECONOMIC TRENDS

Developers see this kind of trend and then develop with more density. That's one reason for an increase in mixed-use projects with residential, retail and office: people are reacting positively to density because it offers convenience. So clearly a market factor like high gas prices can have both bad and good effects.

Market conditions can impact deals and create competitive situations. Another example can be seen in the fight for corners by drugstores and banks. Why do they want to be front and center instead of in-line? Because the market has rewarded these free-standing concepts. Drugstores started seeing more business when they went to a 14,000-square-foot freestanding format with drive-throughs.

Banks used to all be downtown or in a few suburban locations. Now banks are on every corner. They are one of the most profitable industries today. They fight for the corners because they want the visibility and the access.

These market forces have significantly impeded leasing programs.

Outparcels have become one of the most valuable aspects of a development. Leasing strategies are drawn around them and developments are revised because of them.

The best leasing agents are those who understand market forces. They monitor what is happening. They talk to retailers and ask them how they are being affected. They talk to economic development people and ask if they have seen any kind of slowdown.

Some leasing agents go into restaurants just to see how busy they are. They go into malls just to see how many people have shopping bags. Good leasing agents are students of the market.

Different Types of Leasing in Today's Marketplace

As noted above, retail leasing has become more specialized. There still are leasing agents who handle general retail brokerage—they lease and sell projects *and* represent tenants.

The specialists, however, are in abundance. They fall into two main categories: project representatives and tenant representatives.

PROJECT REPRESENTATIVES

A project representative handles leasing for a particular shopping center. These are the names you see on leasing signs, the people responsible for marketing the centers. They do more than lease, however. They can be instrumental in formulating a desired tenant mix. They can come in and re-tenant an existing center. They can create a turn-around plan to rescue an ailing center.

Project representatives often specialize in one category of shopping center. These categories include:

- New developments
- Community retail
- Lifestyle retail
- Mall specialists
- Power retail specialists

Some agents specialize in disposition properties, representing those stores vacated by other retailers. They know every retailer in the market that uses vacated spaces to either enter or expand in a marketplace. More often than not, a project rep agent will have expertise in several of these categories—after all, a lifestyle center isn't built on every corner.

TENANT REPRESENTATIVES

The other major category is tenant representation. Tenant reps work on behalf of a specific retailer. They understand that particular retailer's location needs. They handle site selection, then negotiate with landlords on behalf of the retailer. Most tenant reps specialize in one or two categories. For example, there are tenant reps who handle nothing but furniture retailers. Other categories include lifestyle retailers, mom-and-pops, franchisees, big boxes, restaurants—if a category exists, there's a tenant rep for it.

The leasing agents aren't the only ones who specialize—some companies do as well. Some brokerage companies handle only project representation. Others handle only tenant representation.

The other thing to note is that both project reps and tenant reps typically further specialize geographically. Everything is based on market knowledge, and the tighter the specialization, the greater the knowledge. Larger markets, because of the depth and breadth of business available, will offer more opportunities for specialization than smaller markets, where general brokers would be more common, since the volume of business doesn't justify specialization.

2 | Using the Pro Forma to Create Value and Return

John N. Desco, SCSM, SCLS

What Is a Pro Forma?

The pro forma is a forward-looking financial projection, normally presented at the property level. It is a reflection of income, minus the associated expenses and costs necessary to generate that income. A pro forma can be a snapshot in time (which would be a static pro forma) or a projection over several years.

Pro formas are not typically accounting statements and are not governed by generally accepted accounting principles (GAAP). Pro formas are generally presented on a cash basis. Because pro formas are reviewed by many people involved in property ownership, leasing and management as well as lenders and others, they are traditionally compiled in a simple cash measurement. Not everyone understands accounting and the nuances of each company's accounting policies, but everyone understands cash and cash flows. They are the common language of the pro forma.

The pro forma is the financial baseline for a lease or property cash flow. This chapter will explore one regional mall as a case study. The mall was recently acquired by a new owner. It is a 550,000-foot enclosed regional mall with three anchors: Macy's, Dillard's and JCPenney.

The static pro forma for this mall is shown in Figure 1. This is the 1-year snapshot, showing the revenues and the expenses, all coming down to the bottom line, net operating income (NOI), in a consolidated line-item format.

Figure 1

PRO FORMA	Year 1 Dec-2006
Revenues	
Scheduled Base Rental Revenue	4,815
Retail Sales Percent Revenue	336
Expense Reimbursement Revenue	920
Utilities Income – Tenants	1,125
HVAC – Tenants	176
Specialty Leasing	450
Marketing/Promo Income	137
Miscellaneous Rent	31
Telephones/Misc Income	9
Total Potential Gross Revenue	8,000
General Vacancy	0
Collection Loss	(25)
Effective Gross Revenue	7,975
Operating Expenses	
Property Taxes	550
Property/B&M/Terr Insurance	56
CAM	1,252
Non-Recoverable G&A	67
Management Fee	259
Trash	49
Water/Sewer	56
Tenant Electric	1,016
Misc HVAC Repair	36
Marketing Expense	171
Total Operating Expenses	3,513
Net Operating Income	4,462

Figure 2 shows the pro forma for the same property, but projected out over 10 years. While different properties may have different line items, the process will always be the same—revenues less expenses.

Uses of a Pro Forma

Pro formas can be used in leasing decisions, merchandising and re-merchandising, appraisals, loan sizing, budgeting and property valuation for acquisitions and dispositions. Almost any financial evaluation for decision-making at the property should be done by contrasting the pro forma of a proposed course of action with the pro forma of the current property cash flows.

Figure 2

PRO FORMA

	Year 1 Dec-2006	Year 2 Dec-2007	Year 3 Dec-2008	Year 4 Dec-2009	Year 5 Dec-2010	Year 6 Dec-2011	Year 7 Dec-2012	Year 8 Dec-2013	Year 9 Dec-2014	Year 10 Dec-2015
Revenues										
Scheduled Base Rental Revenue	4,815	5,067	5,302	5,780	6,021	6,147	6,140	6,209	6,244	6,270
Retail Sales Percent Revenue	336	356	381	418	417	409	471	533	525	588
Expense Reimbursement Revenue	920	1,058	1,186	1,288	1,382	1,416	1,445	1,486	1,522	1,537
Utilities Income – Tenants	1,125	1,159	1,194	1,230	1,267	1,305	1,344	1,384	1,426	1,469
HVAC – Tenants	176	182	187	193	198	204	211	217	223	230
Specialty Leasing	450	464	477	492	506	522	537	553	570	587
Marketing / Promo Income	137	141	145	160	154	159	164	168	174	179
Miscellaneous Rent	31	32	33	34	35	36	37	38	39	40
Telephones/Misc Income	9	9	10	10	10	11	11	11	11	12
Total Potential Gross Revenue	8,000	8,468	8,916	9,594	9,990	10,208	10,360	10,600	10,735	10,912
General Vacancy	0	0	0	0	(23)	(110)	(107)	(147)	(108)	(114)
Collection Loss	(25)	(27)	(29)	(30)	(31)	(32)	(33)	(34)	(34)	(35)
Effective Gross Revenue	7,975	8,441	8,887	9,564	9,936	10,066	10,220	10,419	10,593	10,763
Operating Expenses										
Property Taxes	550	605	666	699	720	741	764	786	810	834
Property/B&M/Terr Insurance	56	57	59	61	63	64	66	68	70	73
CAM	1,252	1,290	1,328	1,368	1,409	1,452	1,494	1,540	1,586	1,634
Non-Recoverable G&A	67	69	71	73	75	78	80	82	85	87
Management Fee	259	278	295	323	337	343	349	357	364	371
Trash	49	51	52	54	56	57	59	61	63	65
Water/Sewer	56	58	60	62	64	65	67	69	72	74
Tenant Electric	1,016	1,046	1,078	1,110	1,143	1,178	1,213	1,249	1,287	1,326
Misc HVAC Repair	36	37	38	39	41	42	43	44	46	47
Marketing Expense	171	176	182	187	193	199	204	211	217	223
Total Operating Expenses	3,513	3,668	3,829	3,976	4,100	4,218	4,341	4,469	4,599	4,733
Net Operating Income	4,462	4,774	5,058	5,588	5,835	5,847	5,879	5,951	5,994	6,030

Rounded to thousands.

How to Create a Pro Forma

A pro forma can be built with many tools. One of the easiest is by using a Microsoft Excel spreadsheet. Most people use Excel to create pro formas, from the simplest analysis to the most complex, which may have dozens of sheets containing all tenant detail. Excel files are easily transportable, and any user can analyze and evaluate the input quickly.

Another approach to building a pro forma, which is recommended to anyone who is going to do asset management on an institutional-grade property, is using leasehold analysis software such as ARGUS. ARGUS is a very detailed, hard-coded spreadsheet that permits entry of all pertinent information about the individual tenants in a property. It allows total modeling of the property's operations and incorporates all operating expenses and any capital issues. Using software such as ARGUS, a proposed lease can be evaluated in the context of its impact on the overall performance of the property through use of one simple integrated model.

Some people take a much more informal approach to developing a pro forma, using not much more than the back of an envelope. The advantage to this is time and simplicity, but it is really not recommended for a complex proposal. In all these cases, however, the pro forma is simply a model of revenues less expenses.

PROPERTY INCOME
The first component of the property pro forma is income, or the revenue side. This income includes base minimum rents, percentage rents, reimbursement of operating expenses and any other miscellaneous income.

EXISTING TENANT INCOME
It is simple to create an income projection for a current tenant—it can be extrapolated from the existing lease. To do a pro forma involving an existing tenant, there will usually be a great deal of real information about the tenant to draw from. Besides the lease, there generally are billing statements, sales reports and other budget documents that can be used to determine a tenant's existing and future income. Projecting renewal rents is slightly more difficult and is a function of many factors, materially tenant sales and market rents, and may be

restricted if the tenant has an option to renew at a specific rate that is considered below market.

NEW/SPECULATIVE TENANT INCOME

More difficult to project is income for new or speculative tenants, also known as the lease-up portion of the pro forma. This is more painstaking than projecting income for existing tenants, since there is no existing lease to model, and therefore it requires more thought and analysis. Projecting the income potential for different spaces should involve many people on the owner's team—the leasing specialist, the marketing manager and the mall manager in particular, and anyone else knowledgeable about the market or the tenants.

These parties can determine what type of store should be going into a certain space and why the store needs to be there. In addition, they can determine potential sales for tenants and the rents that should be achieved. While many factors will be brought into play, potential rents are generally a function of supply and demand and tenant sales.

If one has space in demand due to location, where a tenant can generate strong sales, higher rents can be sought. On the other hand, less desirable space commands lower rents as a result of lower sales expectations. In all cases, the leasing agent should try to get potential tenants to do an assessment of their sales potential for that location, which would then be compared to the developer's projection and used to determine a proper rent for the space.

The goal is to find a rent rate on which both parties can agree. If both parties agree that the tenant could do $5 million in sales in a given location and if the tenant can afford to pay 5 percent of its sales in rent, then the tenant and landlord might agree on $250,000 in minimum rent ($5,000,000 ¥ 5% = $250,000).

There are other considerations, however. For example, sometimes the risk of opening the store must be shared between the landlord and the tenant. In that case, the owner and tenant might agree that the tenant only pays a percentage rent based on its actual sales (instead of fixed minimum rent)—for example, again 5 percent. From the example above, if the tenant's sales are only $4 million, then the landlord receives only $200,000 in percentage rent. If, however, the sales exceed expectations at $6 million, then the landlord receives $300,000 in percentage rent. This structure has been a more common practice in recent years and is often used as an inducement to get tenants into a center. This is typically not a favorite arrangement with the owner, since it makes projecting rents more difficult before the store opens.

The cost of building the store and potential cash inducements must be factored into a leasing budget as well. Another issue to be considered is timing. When is the store going to open? How long is the lease? Are there going to be options? Are there termination or kickout rights? Each of these issues needs to be factored into a long-term pro forma.

OTHER INCOME

Other income may include revenue items that the property generates from sources other than the permanent tenants. These include temporary or license tenants, vending machine income, promotion and special events revenue, antennae rents, interest income and even late charges.

OPERATING EXPENSE RECOVERIES

Another important income item that must be considered is the property operating expenses that will be reimbursed to the owner by the tenants (also known as expense recoveries). This involves the property operating expenses described below. While this is probably the least exciting part of the pro forma to develop, it is probably one of the most critical aspects because the average regional mall's operating expense recoveries make up one-third of its total gross revenues.

EFFECTIVE GROSS REVENUE

The sum of all these revenue items, less allowances for vacancy and credit loss, is known as the property's effective gross revenue (see Figure 3).

OPERATING EXPENSES

After the income has been determined, it is necessary to deduct the property's operating expenses. These operating expenses include the cost of common area maintenance (CAM), the cost of operations, security, repairs, insurance and utilities, as well as taxes, administrative and marketing expenses. One can be incredibly accurate in base rent projections for existing and new tenants, but failure to accurately assess operating expenses and the impact of leases on a property's op-

Figure 3

Revenues	
Scheduled Base Rental Revenue	4,815
Retail Sales Percent Revenue	336
Expense Reimbursement Revenue	920
Utilities Income – Tenants	1,125
HVAC – Tenants	176
Specialty Leasing	450
Marketing/Promo Income	137
Miscellaneous Rent	31
Telephones/Misc Income	9
Total Potential Gross Revenue	8,000
General Vacancy	0
Collection Loss	(25)
Effective Gross Revenue	7,975

erating expenses will throw the pro forma far off the mark. Figure 4 shows the operating expenses for the example mall.

Developing the pro forma expenses involves estimating costs that are beyond the owner's and retailer's control. These include utilities and insurance expenses, both of which can be difficult to estimate into the future because these costs are influenced by factors outside the property's control.

Figure 4

Operating Expenses	
Property Taxes	550
Property/B&M/Terr Insurance	56
CAM	1,252
Non-Recoverable G&A	67
Management Fee	259
Trash	49
Water/Sewer	56
Tenant Electric	1,016
Misc HVAC Repair	36
Marketing Expense	171
Total Operating Expenses	3,513

TAXES

An additional long-term factor to be considered is changes in real estate taxes. Experience shows that when a property is bought, taxes are likely to get reassessed within 2 to 3 years. Taxes might rise by statute 9 to 10 percent per year for the next 3 to 4 years until they catch up with the new assessed valuation. The pro forma must account for these increases.

SERVICE CONTRACTS

A final item over which one has limited control, yet must be contained in the pro forma, is the cost of service contracts. If it is a newly acquired property, service contracts will tend to be aggressively priced by contractors to get the new assignment. In the next 2 or 3 years, the service contractor may want to recoup its lower initial rate by attempting to raise its costs to the landlord when the contract comes up for renewal. Another issue can be the impact of changes in the Consumer Price Index (CPI), to which many service contracts tie rate increases.

NET OPERATING INCOME

The "first" bottom line of the pro forma is the net operating income (NOI), or the total income less total recurring expenses. In real estate, NOI is the standard for reporting recurring income and expenses on a cash basis. A property's NOI is usually considered to be the most important single factor in determining the property's value.

NET CASH FLOW

The "second" bottom line in a pro forma is net cash flow, which is simply a deduction of nonrecurring expenses, capital and other nonoperational costs from the NOI. To determine the net cash flow, take the net operating income and subtract debt payments, tenant leasing costs, commissions and nonrecoverable capital and nonoperational ownership costs. Net cash flow is the primary number used to determine what cash is left over after all expenses, costs and deductions for the ownership (or equity) returns. These calculations are shown in Figure 5. Some companies may further deduct non-cash items such as depreciation and cost amortization.

Figure 5

Net Operating Income	4,462
Less:	
Leasing & Capital Costs	
Tenant Improvements	651
Leasing Commissions	130
Capital Reserve	272
Total Leasing & Capital Costs	1,053
Net Cash Flow	3,410

Lease Pro Forma

As mentioned at the start of the chapter, pro formas are usually done at the property level. Pro formas can also be done at the individual lease level—these are called lease pro formas. It is the exact same function as a property pro forma, which is simply showing income less applicable incremental expenses. Lease pro formas can be used to compare different lease proposals or structures as well as determining the landlord's return on its investment in the tenant.

The lease pro forma reflects all rents, whether base or percentage rents, as well as operating expense recoveries. It must account for the term of the lease, tenant allowances and any additional costs incurred by the landlord in order to get the tenant's store open.

Pro Formas Used in Incremental Analysis

The pro forma is also used to do incremental analysis for many decisions: leasing, merchandising, redevelopment and buy/sell decisions.

Figure 6 shows an example of how to structure an incremental cash flow analysis. The incremental analysis determines the potential financial change to a property for a proposed course of action. The incremental analysis will include the proposed net cash flows and proposed incremental costs compared against the base case (or "do nothing") net cash flow. The difference between the two cash flows reflects the incremental impact to the property, both in terms of cost and income. This is the only line item that can truly be used for measuring impacts and returns.

Pro Formas Used for Valuations

Several valuation tools can help assess changes in the value of the property. These valuation tools include using direct capitalization ("cap") rates and discounted cash flows with indirect cap rates. Other derived analyses, such as the internal rate of return (IRR) and the return on cost/capital (ROC), can further explain values.

The capitalization rate is the yield that someone is willing to accept on their investment for a given purchase price and a given income

Figure 6

ANCHOR LEASE					
	Year 1	Year 2	Year 3	Year 4	Year 5
Proposed Net Cash Flow	684	4,982	5,204	5,754	5,901
Proposed Additional Costs	(60)	0	0	0	0
Less Base Case Net Cash Flow	(3,866)	(4,644)	(4,865)	(3,100)	(6,014)
Incremental Cash Flow	(3,242)	338	339	2,654	(113)

Internal Rate of Return:	-0.3%
Net Present Value at 12%:	($853)
Year 5 Value Increase with 7.5% Cap Rate:	($1,507)

stream (or NOI). The actual acceptable yield is based upon many factors, such as the investor's assessment of risk/return for the investment (including cost of funds), the quality of tenants and their sales, location and competition, as well as what the next investor is willing to pay.

The basic relationship of cap rates, income and price is as follows:

NOI ∏ Purchase Price = Capitalization Rate
NOI ∏ Capitalization Rate = Purchase Price
Purchase Price ¥ Capitalization Rate = NOI

Derived Analysis

In addition to static valuation tools, most analyses will include a time-value calculation to analyze the cash flows over time. This is a kind of cash flow analysis in which the net present value of the cash flows is calculated, and/or the internal rate of return is determined. These calculations take into account the time value of money and are considered the most accurate way to determine and compare investment alternatives.

Unfortunately, the actual time-value formulas are fairly complex and should best be calculated using the preset formulas in an Excel spreadsheet or a financial calculator such as a HP-12C.

Case Study in Remerchandising

Any re-leasing of space can take different approaches. Figure 7, on page 28, demonstrates the financial outcomes of two different approaches to remerchandising a space currently occupied by a food court as well as additional common areas at the entrances.

Merchandising Plan 1 imagines the space used by a jeweler, shoe store, sportswear store and destination restaurant. This combination would bring in $332,727 in base rents, but would require $903,200 in tenant allowances and landlord work.

Merchandising Plan 2 looks at the same space as it might be leased to two apparel stores and a less iconic restaurant. Here, base rents

Figure 7

FOOD COURT / ENTRY COURT REMERCHANDISING

Merchandising Plan 1

Use	Area	Rent/sq. ft.	Rent	Cost
Jeweler	1,600	55.00	$88,000	$100,000
Shoes	1,330	22.00	$29,260	$50,000
Sports Apparel	3,830	18.50	$70,855	$153,200
Restaurant	8,034	18.00	$144,612	$600,000
Total	14,794		$332,727	$903,200

Merchandising Plan 2

Use	Area	Rent/sq. ft.	Rent	Cost
Apparel	2,930	24.00	$70,320	$219,750
Restaurant	3,830	18.50	$70,855	$287,250
Apparel	8,034	16.00	$128,544	$125,000
Total	14,794		$269,719	$632,000

would total $269,719, with $632,000 being spent in tenant allowances and improvements.

Comparing the two, Merchandising Plan 1 is more profitable for the landlord. While $271,200 more would be spent on tenant allowances, the revenue differential of $63,000 more than makes up for that over time, and if the property were sold today at a cap rate of 10 percent, the increase in property value of $630,000 ($63,000 ∏ .10) far exceeds the additional tenant allowance investment of $271,000.

Figure 8 shows the impact of Merchandising Plan 1 on the originally budgeted property cash flows over time. This analysis indicates an 18.4 percent return on its incremental investment. The

Figure 8

FOOD COURT / ENTRY COURT REMERCHANDISING

	Year 1	Year 2	Year 3	Year 4	Year 5	Year 6
Proposed Net Cash Flow	3,871	3,723	5,230	3,444	6,340	6,326
Proposed Additional Costs	0	0	0	0	0	0
Less Base Case Net Cash Flow	(3,866)	(4,644)	(4,865)	(3,100)	(6,014)	(6,003)
Incremental Cash Flow	5	(921)	365	344	326	323

Internal Rate of Return: 18.4%

Net Present Value at 12%: $109

Year 6 Value Increase with 7.5% Cap Rate: $4,307

food/anchor court conversion to the jeweler, shoe store, sportswear store and destination restaurant is done over the course of a year and the greatest costs take place in year 2, when the stores are finished and open. Despite that, this merchandising plan shows a positive financial result, which can only be demonstrated with a time value analysis. The incremental analysis indicates this merchandising plan can add more than $4 million of value to the property over time.

Hold/Sell Analysis

Pro formas can also be used to develop an analysis to determine whether to hold or sell a property, as is shown in Figure 9. Timing is an important component in this type of analysis. The goal is to show, based upon the pro forma projections, the best time to sell an investment based upon how much return can be generated to the owner by holding the property for one additional year.

The time-series analysis shows the incremental return on a prop-

Figure 9

HOLD / SELL ANALYSIS (Simple/Unleveraged)

	Year 1	Year 2	Year 3	Year 4	Year 5
Pro Forma NOI	4,975	5,852	6,140	6,407	6,606
Property Value at 7.5% Cap Rate	66,333	78,027	81,867	85,427	88,080
Less Basis	(45,000)	(45,000)	(45,000)	(45,000)	(45,000)
Implied Equity	21,333	33,027	36,867	40,427	43,080

		Year 2	Year 3	Year 4	Year 5
Incremental NOI		877	288	267	199
Incremental Equity		11,693	3,840	3,560	2,653
Incremental Holding Period Return		12,570	4,128	3,827	2,852
Internal Return on Basis of	**$45,000**	**27.9%**	**9.2%**	**8.5%**	**6.3%**

erty bought for $45,000,000. In year 2 of the investment, the total return to the owner (which is measured as the year's net cash flow plus the incremental change in the property value) is 27.9 percent. In year 3, the return for holding one more year falls to 9.2 percent, in year 4 to 8.5 percent and in year 5 to 6.3 percent.

Hypothetically, an investor may be looking for a yield of 7.5 percent. This analysis shows that the property would be attractive to the investor to hold through year 4. In year 5, the incremental return for holding the investment one more year (6.3 percent) falls beneath the annual yield that the investor requires. The conclusion would be to sell in year 4.

Generally speaking, if an owner can show increasing return on a property from year to year, he or she should hold the asset until the yield from holding it one more year falls below the owner's return requirements.

Conclusion

Pro formas play an integral part in the evaluation of most property and lease decisions. Used honestly and correctly, pro formas can provide the direction for the creation of value and returns for any property.

3 Prospecting for Tenants

Heather L. Herring

Understanding Site and Center

Prospecting for tenants is first an exercise in understanding one's site and one's shopping center. Many questions need to be answered. For example, where is the plan for the center going? Is it under redevelopment? Has the project been dying and needs rejuvenation? Or is the goal merely to fill up some space? Has the center undergone expansions or renovations? What is its history?

OWNERS

It is also essential to know the owners and their goals for the center. What are the owners' expectations for leasing? Do they seek permanent leasing deals? Do they want representatives to negotiate? Do they see the agents as just bringing them prospects to be turned over to leasing executives for the final deal?

These are relevant questions because many retailers have been in the business for a very long time. Many of them will know the center in question quite well. Anyone who is prospecting for tenants must know the property at least as well as the target retailer.

RENOVATIONS AND EXPANSIONS

They may know, for example, whether the center has been brought to a new level and really stepped up, or if it also has changed in other ways. What have been its major tenant losses? Has the center lost an anchor or a major tenant?

TENANT ATTRITION

One also needs to understand the many changes in retailing over time. Many retailers have consolidated, many have gone out of business. Have they changed location criteria, from strip centers to regional malls, for example, or vice versa?

CUSTOMER OR RETAILER PERCEPTION

As important as all the factors above is understanding customer perceptions of the shopping center. Is it a great, vibrant center? Is it a center that people avoid because it lacks the latest and greatest? Is the public's memory of a center outdated—are they remembering a run-down center that has been rejuvenated and revitalized?

SALES HISTORY

One needs to know numbers as well as perception. What is the center's sales history? What does the center do now in sales per square foot? Is it better or worse than before?

This kind of information becomes especially important when shopping center construction hits a lull, as it did after the 9/11 attacks. Retailers were looking more than ever to minimize risk. In those situations, potential tenants might only choose to go into a center with a proven sales history. They will very likely know how the center performs and it's sales history, and use that to estimate future sales.

LOCATION

Retailers will also ask how the center relates to the market. Is the center in the growing part of the market? Is it in the dynamic growth area?

ACCESS

There will be plenty of questions about traffic and access. Are there going to be traffic improvements, enhancements in the roads or intersections? Is another mall planned in the area, perhaps with better vehicular access? What are the parking ratios? Where would this tenant be placed in terms of entrances? In lifestyle centers, can customers pull up and park in front of the store? Is the center truly a destination center, or is it focused principally on shopping itself?

VISIBILITY

Visibility is another issue. Can customers see the center from the street? Does construction on outparcels or pads or peripherals block the view of the core shopping center? This is directly related to access and customer perception.

MERCHANDISE PLAN

Examine the current merchandising plan of the shopping center. What types of tenants are already in place? Why are they there? Are they happy in the center? What types of tenants are sought? What changes are desired in the merchandising mix?

Fundamentally, the merchandising mix of a center must be based on trends and must include retailers and services that fill the needs forecast by these trends. This can prove complicated, especially since lease-up of a new center can last 12 to 18 months, with tenant build-out taking 3 to 4 months, meaning that the merchandising mix can be out of step by up to 2 years when the center opens.

A center's merchandise mix should also be unique within the market, giving the shopper a reason to pick that particular center. Centers in very competitive markets will, however, often have to duplicate certain store types since a customer will expect to find particular lines of merchandise in any strip center, any mall, and so on. The mix almost always blends national with local retailers, as well as new and familiar names.

Leasing representatives will also need to examine how the stores will relate to one another. Are there cases where similar types of stores should be grouped together? Are other stores best kept apart? How will destination tenants (those primary to the shopper's focus) interface with the smaller secondary tenants around them?

Finally, in terms of visibility and merchandising, the shopping center should regularly reevaluate its marketing materials. Do they reflect what the center was, what it is or what it wants to be? Do the marketing materials and the center's own vision attract the great locals, the great mom-and-pops and the great franchisees?

Understanding Customer Needs and Demands

What are the needs and wants of customers and potential customers? To answer these questions, marketing people and leasing people should be working together. It is entirely possible that in a given market, customers may want one given type of store but really need another. They may want an upscale brand or retailer, but need a much different retail use or concept. Likewise, a particular retailer may not be as desirable as another with the same product line.

Customer needs and demands extend beyond type of store. Customers also have needs in terms of price points and shopping ambience. They may also have lifestyle requirements—valet parking, accommodating children's needs, and so on.

Understanding Market Demographics

Prospecting for tenants also requires deep and wide understanding of a market's demographics. What is the trade area? How has it changed in recent years? Has it grown or declined? How have the market's income, population and age changed? Are those changes good or bad, given the center's vision and goals? How do the changes enable the center to do something different—think outside the box? That is the crux of prospecting for tenants: finding something new and different.

More often than not, a trade area is not a ring or circle with *x*-mile radius. It can be any type of polygon. The trade area might best be defined as where a center has an identity. It may be a measure of drive time rather than purely mileage. Some markets have a drive time of 5 minutes; for others, it may be an hour.

PSYCHOGRAPHICS AND SOCIOECONOMICS

Demographics are more than simply numbers. A center's demographics track who people are, and the statistics in that trade area. Who, for example, has gone to what level of college, high school, and so on? What is the age range in the market? What proportion of people are married and single? How many have children? What is the average income and average household income versus the medians?

Just as important as behavior and lifestyle choices is how people apply their income—how they spend their money, not just how much. Many areas are appealing on paper and have impressive income and educational levels, but people in that trade area might not have much disposable income. That type of market might present problems for many centers.

Another area worth examining in preparing to prospect for tenants is psychographics and socioeconomics. These reflect the impact of culture and ethnicity on sales. How are those issues going to affect sales, buying power and merchandise mix? Sometimes the issues of culture and ethnicity are positive factors, and sometimes they are negative ones. People shop partially based on norms established in their family and their culture—what they feel is important based on their economic position. For example, markets where many families live in the same home might have more disposable income, since a smaller proportion of income is invested in housing. In some countries, such as Mexico, mortgages and loans are uncommon—families own their homes and therefore may have more disposable income than counterparts elsewhere. In some areas of the United States, of course, many people are mortgaged, exceeded the limit on their credit cards and heavily in debt—there is not as much free spending among that segment. All this affects the potential sales of a store or type of store.

Competition

Competition is also relevant in prospecting for retailers and should not be underestimated. One should not misjudge the competition's ability to come back and remerchandise when they see changes under way, be they in a new center, a renovation or a repositioning in how a center is merchandised.

How one conducts oneself, especially when the heat is turned up in a competitive marketplace, reflects on one's reputation—a matter not to be underestimated when prospecting for tenants. If someone fails to behave in a fair and professional manner, word gets out fast in the industry. This is another reason why knowing the shopping center and its market are all-important—relationship and reputation can rest on data rather than conjecture.

The industry as a whole is more transparent than ever. This affects relationships and reputations, but also information and knowledge. Many developers, for example, now have Web sites that will give specifics on their marketing packages, their plans and how they determine their trade areas. This can help in assessing the competition.

Competition can also come indoors, in a sense. Competition—conscious or not—can exist among those involved with leasing for the same company. All parties need to understand who within a company can lease what space. It is not unheard of for two people from the same company—e.g., someone doing in-line leasing and another leasing to temporary tenants—to approach the same retailer simultaneously. This can significantly affect the profitability of the deal, since leasing is different for temps as opposed to multiyear tenants.

Evaluating Space Requirements and Availability

DETERMINE SPACE AVAILABILITY

In looking at a prospective tenant, the leasing rep must consider what size and kind of space would best suit this retailer and whether the center have that type of space available. A typical retail store has approximately 1 foot of frontage for every 3 to 4 feet of store depth. If available stores are noticeably deeper than that, perhaps it makes sense to split the space so the back of the store can be reoriented to the mall's exterior.

DETERMINE OPTIONS FOR THE SPACE

While a vacant storefront may look like mere space to the untrained eye, the leasing rep sees sales potential there. If the prospective tenant is meant as a destination retailer, for example, the leasing rep might try to find space at a corner for the added visibility. In some cases, the store site could enhance a cluster of similar or complementary stores, creating a "district" within the center. If a space is in an underutilized section of the center, perhaps a food or boutique store could liven up that section. In each case, the overall leasing goals and merchandising mix will affect leasing choices, but the experienced rep will also rely on creative leasing strategies to enhance overall sales.

Creating the Optimum Merchandising Plan

DEFINE CURRENT TENANTS, CATEGORIES AND USES

To re-lease an existing mall, one of the first tasks of a leasing rep is to secure the list of current tenants and examine what merchandise categories they represent. Are certain merchandise trends or brands not represented among the center's tenants? Would these "work" in this particular center?

It is helpful as well to look at lease expiration dates, even within the various categories. If many stores' leases within a given category expire at nearly the same time, it gives the leasing rep an opportunity to reconfigure the merchandising mix of the center to match current shopper needs.

Within the company, there are many bits and pieces that need to be understood. Are there other deals on the table, for example? How would each affect the merchandising plan? Can spaces be reconfigured if need be? Can tenants be moved to accommodate new stores seeking particular locations?

The general uses of the stores should be studied as well. A lifestyle center, for example, might seek stores with high entertainment, food or style value. A center focused on low price points might be more concerned with a broad range of merchandise types, since price, not specialization, would attract shoppers. Generally, do the uses of the store spaces match the overall identity sought by the center?

IDENTIFY KEY TENANTS

Inevitably, some tenants are more important than others to the center's success. In an existing center, this can be determined by sales. In a new center, a key tenant might be defined by the brand's overall sales history or the emergence of favorable merchandising trends. In either case, identifying key tenants (and securing the landlord's agreement with those judgments) will inform the leasing rep's outreach and negotiations. Typically the leasing rep will seek the key tenants first. Depending on the importance of the particular store, the leasing rep may offer a more desirable economic deal, with more allowances or a better rent, to the prospective key tenant.

PREEXISTING USE CLAUSES IN CENTER

Before beginning to contact prospective tenants, the leasing rep will need to determine if the leases of any current tenants (or already contracted tenants in a new center) contain preexisting use clauses. Typically, these clauses allow tenants to be the sole purveyor of a particular kind of merchandise. Obviously, such clauses would affect leasing to other tenants.

Some use clauses only prevail if the store has been exceeding certain sales goals. If a store has been failing to meet those goals, the leasing rep may take advantage of that shortfall and invite a competing store into the center, perhaps as a way to stimulate more creative merchandising by the earlier store or a sales synergy from the presence of competition.

Pinpointing Prospects

Center managers should define the various categories of stores they already have. What types of stores are missing? Are some tenants underperforming? Is the center oversaturated with a particular category of retailer—eight or nine cell phone stores, five or six nail salons?

Making these assessments is difficult enough, but relationships get complicated when reconfiguration begins. Tenants often feel they need to be near this store or that one. If reconfiguration will affect a tenant, it is important for anyone working with that tenant to explain how the new plan will benefit that tenant. Perhaps the new synergy will improve on the old. All this, of course, needs to fit in with the center's overall goals.

It is very useful to visit other shopping centers, including those in other cities, to see their design how they function. The various arrangements of retailers would probably be the major topic of study, but one can also look at vehicular access, entertainment attractions, food venues and other aspects. One should always pick up maps and mall directories on those visits, particularly since it will provide lasting evidence of a prospective tenant's neighbors in other cities' malls.

MATRIX OF OPTIMUM PROSPECTS IN EACH CATEGORY

A chart or Excel spreadsheet can be helpful in analyzing the merchandising mix in the existing shopping center. It can be organized by categories—fast food, fashion apparel, children's wear, unisex, juniors, accessories, etc. Once the trade area's demographics and spending patterns have been assessed, it is a relatively simple matter to identify the ideal store in each merchandise category and see whether it is part of the current mix or the mix that is sought.

Canvassing

RESOURCES

Before the contact, the leasing rep gets information. Vast information resources are available to assist in this effort. The Internet has transformed the leasing process, and ICSC.org provides a plethora of information. Retailers' own Web sites are very useful, with many specifics on their marketing programs.

Networking at industry events and conferences is helpful, as are shopping center directories and publications. Other good tools for canvassing include the local chamber of commerce, economic development organizations, and, yes, the Yellow Pages. Brokers and tenant representatives can also be useful sources—one should always, however, discuss fees with them up front.

DETERMINE THE CORRECT CONTACT

Once all this information has been secured, one can work on making the contact, which should be as personal as possible. E-mail is often abused a lot in this process. Leasing people learn quickly that the most efficient way to make the initial contact is in person. Walk into the store and ask for the manager—this is a particularly good way to meet the locals.

When reaching out to a national retailer, call the company. Most leasing reps wisely avoid e-mails for an initial contact. They also do not send blind packages with a letter. Experienced leasing reps call the company, offer a name and a voice, personalize the relationship and set up a face-to-face meeting whenever geography will permit.

This is not to dismiss e-mail, but it should be used only after the relationship has been established. It is good to remember that anything put in an e-mail is actually put in writing—deal terms, negotiations, and so forth. Those should all be done after, not before, a personal relationship has been forged.

Arranging a Site Visit

Visiting other local shopping centers provides information of a brass-tacks nature. For starters, it can verify whether a particular chain has a store nearby. Also, a new retail format may be examining several shopping centers in a given market. A good look at the competition will point up the advantages of one's own center. Does the competing center have enough customer amenities, accessibility or parking? Is the signage and lighting as good? All these aspects contribute to sales and revenue and are part of the equation for retailers considering new locations.

Prerequisites to Signing a Deal

Creating a personal relationship also helps determine whether the retailer is qualified to lease space. In the case of an independent, does the retailer have a business plan? If not, one might advise them of the usefulness of a plan, and call back when it is done—in those cases, the retailer is really being guided into a leasable situation. Does the retailer have a sales history? A financial statement?

FINANCIAL STATEMENTS

The issue of financial statements can be particularly tricky. A lot of national retailers have multiple identities—different corporations, different regions, and so on. Whichever entity is signing the lease is the one whose financial statement should be examined.

There are many other reasons for a thorough vetting of ownership and finances, not the least of which are new federal laws related to terrorism. A center is required in the lease documents to verify their information.

One should also be cautious of completely independent retailers and those just starting to incorporate, since they may have little liability if they go out of business. When a store is owned by a married individual, make sure both the husband and wife sign if the state has community property laws.

Make sure there is a guarantor and security deposits. These demonstrate the retailer's commitment to the deal, and they should all be part of the lead-up to the lease signing.

SALES HISTORY

Just as the leasing rep examined the sales history of the shopping center (see above), the sales history of the prospective tenant must be determined. What has happened in recent years to the company's overall sales? Are consumer trends favoring this tenant? Does the merchandise line benefit from current demographic trends? What has been the brand's sales experience in this market or those nearby? Does this brand do better in one particular type of center or another?

BASIC REQUIREMENTS OF RETAILERS

In return for signing the lease, what is the retailer getting? Is the owner going to do landlord work and construction? Will the owner give them an allowance? Can the owner terminate the lease—and if so on what terms? Is the retailer required to repay construction costs? What marketing support will the landlord give? What demographic information can the owner hand off to the retailer, since he or she will probably report back to a committee? Many of these issues should be part of the pro forma.

Clearly, prospecting for tenants is a two-phase activity—first information, then contacts. The information serves to benefit both the tenant and owner—both must go into a leasing deal sharing the same knowledge. Yet the best information in the world will not pay off without a personal relationship based on ethical, honest and professional behavior, to build the foundation for lease negotiations in the years to come.

4

The Art of the Deal

Steven W. Toppel, CLS

The Leasing Representative

Leasing representatives come from many backgrounds and a wide variety of academic disciplines. Success as a leasing rep comes more from one's personality type than from training. Someone who is disciplined, gregarious, motivated and loves a challenge stands a good chance of success. However, in this real estate industry, 75 percent of one's efforts usual result in rejection, so the leasing rep must stay focused on goals and objectives and keep a positive attitude. One of the best ways to describe this industry is a "people business." Establishing and maintaining good relationships is paramount to the longevity and continued success of a leasing repesentative.

FUNCTIONS OF THE LEASING REP

Leasing representatives are deal makers but can also be described as facilitators. They are also considered the gatekeepers of their shopping center properties. They are usually the first people retailers talk to when they want an opportunity to open a new store.

As facilitators, they negotiate the business issues but do not have final approval rights and rarely have the authority to sign lease documents. Leasing reps understand the budget expectations and guidelines, but they are not the final decision makers—those decisions are usually made by corporate committees at higher asset management positions. Therefore, leasing reps must also keep a realistic perspective on their work. No matter how much work a leasing rep puts into a deal, it may be negated from within the company for a myriad of reasons.

A typical leasing rep is responsible for multiple shopping center properties totaling millions of square feet of space. At any given time, there are dozens of deals in negotiations and leases awaiting signatures. On an ongoing basis, leasing reps interact with their retail counterparts or consultants, tenant coordinators, attorneys, asset managers and shopping center management teams to finalize deals.

The primary function of a leasing rep is production. With the goal of adding value to a property. As an example, negotiating a deal that generates $100,000 of base minimum rent (given a 10 percent capitalization rate) equates to $1 million in added value. Income generated by the leasing rep transfers directly into the value of the center. Leasing reps also develop budgets and merchandising plans, identify tenant prospects and often act as new business liaisons. They work to increase and improve co-tenancy through merchandising and remerchandising.

Essential to the success of a leasing rep is the portfolio to which he or she is assigned. There is a direct correlation between the quality and desirability of a property and the productivity of the rep. If, however, the property has high occupancy with minimal lease expirations, the rep's productivity will be limited.

Regardless of the type of portfolio one has, one must have comprehensive knowledge of the property and a vision for improvement. The rep must identify additional opportunities to enhance the portfolio. Which existing tenants can be replaced with better-producing ones? How can the center's vacancy rate be cured with an advantageous merchandising plan?

This is challenging for an experienced rep, and the challenge is amplified for a new leasing rep. It takes time to learn the markets, retailers, categories, leasing negotiating terms and techniques. Therefore, it is most beneficial to have a mentor—usually a senior leasing rep—assigned to the junior rep to guide the new rep through the process in the early years of work.

If you compare the leasing business and training of junior leasing reps to the military, there is a huge difference. In the military, no one is sent into harm's way until he or she is fully trained—boot camp, specialized training and schools, etc. The mall leasing business, however, does not offer such a structured learning environment—there is limited time to devote to the junior reps. The senior reps are usually focused on maximizing their own productivity. In most instances, the junior leasing rep is assigned a portfolio and expected to produce. Adroit junior reps will seek out a mentor and learn the business through the mentor's guidance and experience.

The mentor will provide the nucleus of information and illustrate how success in the art of the deal grows from knowledge, negotiating and people skills. Leasing reps need to understand the variables of a deal, how other disciplines interact with leasing, and the very latest trends in retailing and consumer needs. One must think of the deal as being about the retailers' needs and goals. What do they require for the deal to work? What will make a comprehensive and successful negotiation process for all parties involved?

PROPERTY TYPES

Generally, shopping center leasing reps deal with two property types: enclosed malls and open-air lifestyle centers. In either case, this type of property will be a new center under construction (from the ground up) or an existing center, where vacancies need to be filled and underproducing retailers replaced.

MERCHANDISING VS. LEASING

Apart from physical differences, the two types of center usually differ in their merchandising. What works in one type of center may not work in another. The good leasing rep is a student of retail, and many questions need to be examined. Who/what are the retail and service concepts—not just the retailers', but the other centers? What/how are they doing and with whom? What are their price points? How do they fit in the center? What is the sales productivity in the other centers? One needs to look beyond category. A rep may seek an apparel store to occupy a space, but a discount apparel store might not enhance the merchandising mix of the property.

Another area to be aware of is bankruptcies. The rep must know when certain tenants are at risk of or considering Chapter 11. When a retailer goes into bankruptcy, the owner must consider recapture of space. This creates an opportunity not only for increasing rent with a backfill tenant, but also remerchandising the center with a better retailer.

One must also know what restrictions and rules have been imposed by the center's anchor deals—the reciprocal easement agreements (REAs). Typically, when a center is developed, each department store owns its own land. The department store usually imposes restrictions as to what an owner cannot do and to whom the owner cannot lease.

Many of these rules are common sense—the agreement may say the owner cannot rent to bingo halls, for example. Some, however, include restrictions that might affect how the center is merchandised and leased—these REAs must be available and known to the rep.

INFORMATION SOURCES

The rep needs to understand what retailers do and how they do it. As a student of this industry, the rep has numerous publications available; for example, a weekly called *The Deal Maker*. Within this publication the rep will find the latest transactions—who is hot, who is not and what is happening nationwide. ICSC's products and services— its magazine *Shopping Centers Today*, ICSC's Web site and publications— are valuable resources. ICSC conventions are a useful resource—the *Registration Book* is current and provides full contact information within the shopping center and retail industries.

KNOWLEDGE OF MARKET, CENTER AND COMPETITION

Leasing reps also must be continuing students of market demographics. Armed with this information, the rep can provide retailers with information needed to support the deal—evidence needed by their leasing counterpart on the retailer side.

A well-defined trade area will assist the retailers with their statistical analyses. For example, the retailer will want to know income levels—usually per capita and per household. The retailer will also want to know how that income level is changing over time—is it rising or falling? A high-end retail tenant will not want to locate in a mall where per capita income is low and declining further.

Based on the retailer's target customer, other demographic considerations might be primary. Age would be a key issue for a children's retail store. The retailer would view this in terms of numbers/age of children in the area and who shops for these children.

The rep also will need to know whether the same stores exist in the well-defined trade area. The retailer will not want to cannibalize from existing sales and want to maintain a certain distance. Also, these existing stores may have radius restrictions contained in their existing lease that prevent opening a store in another project. The radius restriction is a negotiated distance wherein the retailer cannot open another store of the same brand name.

The rep also needs to know the area's competition. On a map illustrating the trade market, the locations of every competitive center should be identified. Retailers will want to see where their existing stores are located within the trade area and where the competing stores are. The rep also should be familiar with the sales figures of those competing stores. The success or weakness of these stores may influence the rep's attitude toward offering a location within his or her center.

The rep also should have two types of center plans. The first is a site plan. It shows the total view of the exterior property, not just the main mall/shopping center building. This includes outparcels, parking, dock-loading areas, trash enclosures, and access roads, etc. The second plan is called a lease plan. This illustrates all the spaces inside the mall/shopping center occupied by tenants, including each entrance, stairs, escalators, elevators, common areas, center court, food court, restrooms, offices, storage, and rear access corridors.

One of the most dynamic opportunities for a leasing representative is the assignment to lease a brand-new project from the ground up or to lease a comprehensive redevelopment. This type of assignment is effectively a clean slate. Hundreds of thousands of square feet are available to lease. The rep has complete flexibility and creativity. Prior to redevelopment, it may be difficult to see the initial opportunities and vision. Perhaps the site is run-down, or a bad layout, or has other disadvantages—but the time is right for a comprehensive change. This is another reason why market research and demographics play a vital role to support such an expensive undertaking.

Commitment from anchors will often determine how a new center is merchandised. An anchor is typically viewed as a department store, with junior anchors being a large bookstore, theater, and so on. If the anchors are Neiman Marcus and Nordstrom, the leasing rep has a good opportunity to merchandise with more upscale retailers and luxury stores. If the anchors are Sears, Dillard's and JCPenney, the retail lineup will be more moderate.

SECURING A TENANT

Leasing to anchors, junior anchors and retailers requires the rep to build relationships. These relationships often last for years, sometimes decades. Managed properly, they will be the foundation for many future leasing deals. These relationships are a crucial component to the art of the deal.

The relationship builds from the basic social niceties to a trusting level between the leasing rep and the retailer. An initial conversation often leads to a site tour of a particular property or trade market. This includes introducing retailers to a new or changing trade area, property and space inspection, and providing a compelling reason to proceed with a deal.

Some developers host social events for retailers and occasionally include other developers in the market, where certain information—not proprietary information—can be shared in a quick, informal setting.

Deal Structure

The economics of each deal must be acceptable to both landlord and retailer. In addition, there are provisions that are usually addressed prior to submission of a deal (i.e., early termination, co-tenancy, radius restrictions, etc.). Representatives of both parties will need to present the proposed terms of the deal to committees at their respective companies. The proposed deal will need to stand up to committee expectations and questions. Both representatives (landlord and tenant) at the deal-making level should explain to each other what their respective committees will require. If a good relationship exists, the reps will cooperate to support each other's presentations. This will allow for a more thorough presentation and optimize the chances of approval.

The deal structure presented to the committees contains specific terms to be inserted into a new but standardized lease document. These would include:

- Date
- Name, address and contact information for the proposed tenant
- Size and the space number of the tenant space
- Permitted use of the space
- Turnover date for the space
- Rent commencement date
- Term of the lease
- Minimum annual rent
- Percentage rent rate
- Radius restriction
- Operating expenses, broken out by category
- Any special provisions

A major point of negotiation may come up in defining the permitted use of the space. The permitted use of the space must be defined in order to establish the approved parameters to operate the business during the term of the lease. The landlord wants this language to be as tight and restrictive as possible. On the other hand, the retailer may want the permitted use to be as generic as possible, using fairly ambiguous language. For example, the store or chain may want to add a product line—perhaps a jeans store wants to sell CDs to its younger clientele. The mall, however, may already have a music store whose lease grants it exclusivity in selling music. Resolving those conflicts between the two leases could prove a costly undertaking for the owner. Therefore, the permitted use clause always takes precedence and establishes the guidelines for all tenants.

The turnover date and the rent commencement dates are different. The turnover date is when delivery of possession occurs. The rent commencement date is either when the tenant opens for business or a firm date stated in the lease document. Upon delivery of possession, the tenant is granted a period of time to complete the store's construction/buildout. Typically, the turnover date will allow for 60 to 90 days before the rent commencement date. Sometimes, however, the plan approval process or the permitting process will stall. Thereafter, the rent commencement date will be delayed unless stated in the lease document as previously mentioned.

The landlord rep and the tenant rep negotiate the proposed rent. The landlord rep should never be afraid to offer an aggressive rent, but should also have a compelling story to justify the proposal. Before the tenant rep can respond, he or she usually requires a sales estimate from the retailer's operations department. Based on the projected sales volumes and rent-to-sales ratio, the tenant rep will respond accordingly. Regardless of the value the landlord places on its lease space, the tenant can only pay what it believes will be supported through projected sales.

Another variable to increase rent may occur through percentage rent. This is only paid to the landlord when the tenant's gross sales exceed the percentage rent breakpoint. The percentage factor is defined in the lease and varies from tenant to tenant. Percentage rent allows the landlord to share in the tenant's success. The percentage rent clause will include a breakpoint—a specific annual sales amount. If sales exceeds this amount each year, the negotiated percentage above the breakpoint is paid to landlord. Example: if the breakpoint is $500,000, annual sales are $600,000, and the percentage factor is 6 percent, the landlord is entitled to 6 percent above $500,000 or $6,000 in percentage rent.

Another term used is the "net effective rent." It is determined by adding the percentage rent (also known as "overage rent") to the base rent. The resulting net effective rent comes into play at lease renewal time. The owner will try to get the new base rent to equal the current net effective rent, knowing that in negotiations the number will probably drop between 80 to 90 percent of the net effective rent as the new base rent. This can vary if the retailer, for example, has had an exceptional final year prior to lease renewal.

A tenant allowance is paid to the tenant to help offset the construction costs of the new store. This is often available to national retail tenants with strong financial statements. The stronger the statement, the less risk involved. If a retail tenant has a weak financial statement, the risk is higher and that tenant is unlikely to receive an allowance.

Issues That Make or Break Deals

In addition to the basic economic terms and conditions of a deal, there are other issues of significant importance. The right to relocate a tenant is very important to landlord and tenant. The purpose of this provision is to allow the landlord to control the real estate after a lease document is fully executed. On the other hand, a tenant agrees to commit to a specific space throughout the term of the lease because of its location in the mall. Lease documents have a provision allowing for the landlord's right to relocate the tenant. Most sophisticated tenants will either attempt to strike this provision or establish a defined relocation zone in the event of relocation. In addition, the tenant will require a comparable size and specified condition of space. In the event a suitable space is not available at time of relocation, lease termination often results, with a buyback payment from the landlord to the tenant. This buyback helps the tenant recuperate its unamortized construction costs.

Many national retailers require a co-tenancy provision. This provision states the number of anchors to remain open for business during their lease term and a percentage of the entire small shop gross leased area (GLA). The primary reason a store seeks a mall location is the drawing power of the center; ie, its anchors and the small shop tenants. Each retailer needs to be protected against the possibility of one or more anchors closing, or a large number of store closures. Such action would reduce the center's draw and negatively impact the sales of the stores remaining open. Landlords can protect against this by requiring a sales test—evidence that the store's sales have actually suffered by the closings. In any event, remedy language in the event of co-tenancy failure will be clearly addressed in the lease document.

Exclusivity is a provision few tenants are granted. All productive malls maintain a proper balance of categories—women's and men's apparel, shoes, jewelry, food, services, accessories, children's, electronics, optical, etc. Clustering tenants and proper merchandising is essential to a successful mall. Too much of any category, however, dilutes sales and adversely affects the productivity of the mall. Granting exclusivity restricts the leasing rep from securing similar tenants and protects the retailer from direct competition. If exclusivity is granted, remedy language will also be clearly addressed in the lease document.

Tenant Issues

In addition to dealing with specific lease provisions, the landlord's lease approval committee will require and review the tenant's financial statement. The financial statement must reflect net worth and liquidity. The strength of these financials will determine the risk of this tenant. Retailers understand the owner's assessment of risk and typically comply with this request as a condition of the deal. The leasing rep must request and obtain this material before the deal is presented to the lease approval committee.

Another component for consideration and review is the lease comparable. Most landlords maintain a database of ongoing and completed lease transactions. This provides a snapshot of the primary economic terms and conditions of other deals with this same tenant. The leasing rep should review this information and compare it to their deal. This will ensure consistency and avoid setting a poor landlord precedent.

Leasing Support

In pursuing a retail concept, the rep should take full advantage of the owner's support divisions, particularly the marketing department and the mall management staff. The marketing department can provide assistance in graphics, demographics, photographs, presentations, etc. The mall management staff usually knows more about the property than does the leasing agent. The mall general manager and the operations director can also provide useful information on the condition of the leasable space and field-verify such things as size, utilities and what will need to be done physically at lease renewal time.

Upon approval by the lease committee, the landlord's attorney will usually draft and send out the lease document. From the attorney's perspective, the most important two words, constantly asked, are, "What if . . . ?" What if the tenant kicks out? What if the retailer is in default? What if there are no relocation spaces? Leasing reps can save time and money if they ask those types of questions of themselves and discuss them with their retail counterparts. Leasing reps need to understand that there is a consequence for every action that can occur in the owner-tenant relationship. Therefore, remedy language must always be addressed whenever the tenant requests exclusivity, early termination, etc.

Once the lease document itself is approved, the tenant coordinator can begin work. The tenant coordinator provides the tenant with construction criteria information and maintains construction review, approval and oversight. The tenant coordinator will work with the tenant from the very beginning to the completion of construction. The tenant coordinator also assists in negotiating the construction exhibit of the lease, reviewing and making suggestions, granting approval of the plans and helping the tenant obtain permits. He or she also produces a checklist, subject to approval by all parties involved, related to construction and operational components. The construction chargeback needs to be well defined. For example, who will pay for barricades to keep shoppers from the construction area? Who will pay for the temporary utilities and the temporary trash service? Who will pay for the sprinkler shutdown during construction? These and other construction costs are negotiable items within the lease, but typically the landlord will seek merely to cover expenses.

Philosophy of Negotiations

With regard to the philosophy of negotiations, all leasing reps have their own style. This is dictated by their life experiences, training, core values and work ethic. One of the most successful negotiating techniques is: "tell a compelling story." Leasing reps should always be able to support their position, justify requests and listen carefully to their counterpart. They do their homework in advance and have all information available at the time of negotiations. They anticipate problems and offer solutions. They leave room to maneuver and make their counterparts feel as though they have been successful.

Leasing reps on both sides are facilitators and have the same goals and objectives. Upon completion of negotiations, both parties will become each other's advocates. Both will present the same deal to their respective committees for approval and therefore have a unique alliance. Cooperation makes the process easier and often enjoyable, which should enhance relationships and enable future business opportunities.

Clearly, the art of the deal rests on many factors such as: economics, the structure of the deal and tenant issues. Most important, however, is the philosophy of how the deal is negotiated. Professionalism, which includes honesty, ethical behavior and courtesy—returning calls, keeping a peer relationship, mutual respect—is at the heart of the deal and can lay the groundwork for productive deal making for many years to come.

5 | The Lease and Its Administration

John L. Gerdes, SCSM, CLS, CPM

There are many ways to negotiate each and every clause within a lease. Lease clauses are affected by the market, real estate law, company policy and other factors. By understanding a few basics and applying a bit of logic, the leasing agent can usually come up with a solution to any impasse reached in the leasing process. Once done, the lease is always the rule to follow, although lease interpretation may vary.

Protecting Clauses

While leasing representatives arrange deals, they also are responsible for protecting lease clauses during the negotiation process. They do so to add value to the lease. Each clause in the lease protects or enhances the income to be derived from the store and, in return, from the property. Each time a key clause is watered down or eliminated at the request of the retailer—or even just omitted in oversight by the landlord's representative—the value of the lease potentially diminishes, producing less income for the landlord. In short, the content and quality of the lease clauses are what make a property work for all parties in the lease.

Enforcing Clauses

The leasing rep and, by inference, the committee that approves the deal are accountable for protecting the lease clauses, but management—the operations team at the mall or center—is responsible for enforcing the clauses.

In the early days of the industry, the landlord could be fairly tough about enforcing lease clauses. There was much tighter enforcement of, for example, lease line requirements, which determine how far past the lease boundaries a store's display can be placed. Mall reps would come by with measuring tapes and push the displays back if they exceeded the lease line. Nowadays, with more competition in the industry and all parties being challenged to increase sales, landlords are likely to be more lenient about these kinds of clauses, in order to keep the tenant happy.

Failing to keep the tenant happy comes back to haunt the landlord, since retailers talk to one another, and word will spread through the mall that the landlord is not responsive to the stores' needs, which can complicate matters at lease renewal time, if not sooner.

What's Important in the Lease and Why

One way to keep retailers satisfied is to have negotiated a good lease—one whose clauses are satisfactory to landlord and tenant alike. There are many important clauses in a lease.

RENT

The base rent must be stated in the lease for it to be a valid contract. Traditionally, the rent was expressed in annual terms, per square foot (for example, $24 per square foot per year). Sometimes the monthly equivalent is expressed as well for clarity (e.g., $2 per square foot per month). Recently, some landlords have stated rents strictly in monthly terms per square foot. Clearly, it is important to express not just the dollars due in rent, but also the frequency. The other type of rent is percentage rent, which will be explored later in this chapter.

Rent based on a per-square-foot basis naturally requires the exact measurement of every tenant space individually and the total square footage of leasable space in the center. This allows the landlord to allocate not only rent but all other charges (CAM, or common area maintenance costs, and real estate taxes) on a pro rata basis related to the percentage of the leased premises as a part of the total leasable square footage.

DATES

The lease must include the commencement date, which is the date on which the rent payments begin. It should include also the termination date, the date on which the lease ends. Throughout the deal negotiations, parties may have been discussing a 10-year lease, for example, but that would mean that a lease signed in the fall might end just before the holiday shopping season, which likely neither party would want. In those cases, the termination date might be 10 years and 2 or 3 months after the commencement date. There are usually ways to adjust the termination timing within the lease document.

The lease also should include the effective date of the lease, which is not necessarily the date on which the lease is signed—the parties may agree within the lease that it is to take effect some weeks or months later. The lease also will likely include the turnover date, which is the date on which the tenant can take possession of the space and begin improvements.

COMMON AREA MAINTENANCE (CAM)

The common area maintenance is the cost of maintaining the common areas of the mall, including walkways, parking lots, restrooms, etc, and what is done to them—cleaning, snow removal, and the like. (See figure 1, CAM, for a sample of one company's definition of the

Figure 1

CAM

"Common area charge" means the landlord's gross actual costs and expenses of every kind or nature incurred by or imposed upon landlord, in or by reason of landlord's ownership, operation, management, maintenance and/or replacement of the common areas, the cost of operating, repairing, heating, lighting, air-conditioning, cleaning, painting, removing snow, ice, leaves and debris, providing off-site parking, providing security, sewage and trash disposal charges, insurance for hazard and other risks and any other insurance landlord deems necessary, licensing fees, a reasonable allowance for the depreciation of, or for the rental of, vehicles and maintenance equipment, direct and payroll overhead and payroll taxes and benefits.

term.) Those costs typically include a 15 percent administrative fee for the oversight and management of CAM. This is calculated as an additional 15 percent on the total cost and added as a line item. In many cases the lease will contain a clause to collect a management fee as a part of CAM as well. Many retailers today are only allowing the landlord to charge one or the other. The retailer position is that the management of the center includes the oversight of CAM and there should be no additional fee.

The total CAM costs of the shopping center are split among the tenants, although the formulas may be different. As mentioned previously, all the leasable areas and the total area of the center need to be specified in the lease, or the landlord will have difficulty in collecting tenants' share of the costs when improvements are undertaken or even for general operation of the center.

Insurance costs and security costs are also usually covered under CAM, and skyrocketing expenses for both items have made it clear that these costs under CAM cannot be expressed purely as a standard percentage increase from the base.

If a tenant is demanding a set cap or limit on the increases in costs for common area expenses, then security, insurance and utilities increases should not be included. In some areas, snow removal may be included as a noncontrollable cost as well. These costs, along with real estate taxes, should be designated as noncontrollable and should be separated from controllable costs whenever possible.

CAM RECOVERY CALCULATION

Basically, common area maintenance costs for each tenant are calculated by dividing the landlord's actual expense of maintaining common areas by the gross leasable area (GLA) to arrive at a per square foot charge. The tenant is then charged the amount equal to that per square foot charge multiplied by the number of square feet occupied by the store, representing its pro rata share. Figure 2 shows a lease provision specifying how CAM can be calculated. Certain types of leasable area may be excluded from that figure, such as an anchor tenant, certain types of specialty stores, or units given to service, convenience or recreation. Typically, however, there is a minimum percentage of the total GLA (perhaps 80 percent) below which the GLA assessment cannot fall. The purpose of the 80 percent factor is to allow the retailer to have some assurance that costs will not increase above a certain level due to the landlord's inability to lease va-

Figure 2

CAM

Tenant's proportionate share of the common area charge, which shall be computed on the ratio which the floor area of the demised premises bears to the total floor area of the shopping center, which is leased, occupied and producing rent, including the demised premises, but excluding floor area landlord designates as anchor tenant and/or specialty store tenant space and space of recreational and convenience uses; provided, however, tenant's share of the common area charge shall be calculated on the basis of not less than eighty percent (80%) of the gross leasable area of the shopping center (excluding anchor tenant space, specialty store tenant space,and space for recreational and convenience uses).

---

cant space. That occupancy section is usually tied to some action in the lease that allows the retailer to have certain rights, whether they are limits on extra charges, reduced rental or even termination of the lease. These clauses should contain a time frame of notice and cure for the landlord to increase the occupancy to a level above the agreed threshold. The clause should always have clear language that reverts whatever penalty was included once the threshold is above the agreed amount.

TAXES

Tax expense, which is also divided among the tenants, is kept separate from CAM costs. A common arrangement is shown in Figure 3, the tenant pays a proportion of the taxes. The proportion is based on the same ratio used in calculating CAM of tenant-occupied square footage versus total leasable square feet of the center. As mentioned previously, real estate taxes (RET) are an uncontrollable expense of the landlord that must be passed on fairly to the tenants. The costs associated with any tax appeals or other efforts to reduce taxes should be included in the overall RET amount passed through. Additionally, there is a lot of work involved from the management staff to prepare, process and handle the RET. Many landlords are able

Figure 3

TAXES

The tenant's share of taxes shall be computed on the ratio that the floor area of the demised premises bears to the total floor area of the shopping center, which is leased, occupied and producing rent including the demised premises but excluding floor area Landlord designates as anchor tenant space and/or specialty store tenant space, and floor area used for post office, child care nursery purposed, or other principally for service, convenience or recreation to customers of the shopping center provided, however, tenant's share of taxes shall be calculated on the basis of not less than eighty percent (80%) of the gross leasable area of the shopping center (excluding anchor tenant space, specialty store tenant space, and space as noted above).

---

to include an administrative fee (similar to CAM) for those efforts in the overall allocation as well.

INSURANCE

Insurance is a mutually required section of every lease between the landlord and the tenant. The lease should specify the insurance carried by both parties and in what limits. Local custom and company policy will often dictate the amounts. Usually there is a clause for general liability insurance from both parties ranging from $1 million to $3 million or more. The indemnification clause will often need to be reviewed closely in conjunction with the insurance clause. The landlord should insist that the tenants list the landlord entity and any other interested landlord parties (i.e., management company) as "additional insureds" on the tenant policy. If an incident occurs within the tenant space, the landlord would prefer to have the tenant's insurance cover the loss and any litigation related to it—thus the need for the landlord to be listed as an additional insured on the tenant policy. Copies of those polices showing the landlord as listed should be kept in the management office and updated regularly. Requiring each tenant to carry its own insurance (and verifying it) also will be important in the case of a loss inside the store that affects the landlord's property or other tenants.

This is another area where defining the separation of the lease line from the common area will clear up a lot of disagreement in the future.

USE CLAUSE

The use clause specifies the purpose(s) to which the leased space can be put. A shopping center's success depends in part on the mix of retailers, which is to say the merchandise available at each store. If retailers were allowed to change the purpose of their stores at will, it would be impossible for the landlord to maintain a viable merchandise mix. A coffee bar should not be allowed to become a juice bar without the landlord's approval. A jeans store should not be permitted to sell compact discs without the landlord's consent. For fast food operations, the actual menu may be part of the use clause, since the landlord does not want to see six food court tenants suddenly selling pizza. Similarly, the landlord may specifically want to preclude similar uses in stores that are side by side or in close proximity. The use clause protects the landlord from these developments.

Figure 4

USE CLAUSES

Permitted uses: Tenant shall use the demised premises only as and for the display and sale at retail of women's apparel, lingerie, swimwear, t-shirts,shoes and accessories including hats, handbags, hosiery, hair goods, belts, cosmetics, beauty products, jewelry, watches, sunglasses, consumables (including candy and soda pop [but vending machines are specifically not allowed]), and miscellaneous gift items including books, stationery, paper goods and scented products. As a condition of this lease, tenant hereby expressly understands and agrees that tenant shall not sell any merchandise and/or apparel from the demised premises of a sexually themed nature, pornographic nature, or drug-related nature (including but not limited to merchandise and/or apparel depicting drugs or slogans promoting the use of drugs) or merchandise depicting crimes and/or commemorating the acts of real life nonfictional criminals or persons accused of or incarcerated for alleged crimes. Tenant shall use the demised premises for no other purpose whatsoever.

EXCLUSIVES

These clauses allow a given tenant to be the only purveyor of a particular type of merchandise in the mall. Clauses for exclusivity usually do not work to the landlord's advantage, since they limit the landlord's options for recruiting other tenants. If clearly and narrowly defined, similar tenants can operate with similar merchandise and actually thrive; however, broad exclusives complicate that arrangement. Though sometimes, exclusives are acceptable to the landlord, particularly in the case of a highly prized tenant. The landlord will get the most advantage from an exclusivity clause in which wording is very precise as to the type, style or manner of business. Vague exclusives will often result in disputes with the tenants and sometimes in litigation. When landlords grant an exclusive, they should carefully consider the effect on the future of the center. If the value of that tenant for competitive or merchandising reasons outweighs the potential conflict, it may well be worth granting the clause. Often such clauses are needed to get highly coveted tenants and can even be used by the landlord to make sure other tenants comply with their own use clauses by inclusion of all exclusives as an exhibit in other tenants' leases.

RADIUS RESTRICTIONS

These clauses prevent a retail chain from opening the same store within a certain distance from the space being leased—for example, the landlord would want to restrict "Josie's Fashions" from opening another store less than 4 miles from the unit being leased. The actual mileage will vary from market to market, dependent on geography, population density, retail development, and so on. The distance will also vary depending on the tenant, its use and its desirability. To enforce these clauses, landlord representatives should visit nearby shopping centers on a fairly regular basis, paying particular attention to retailers that operate out of kiosks or other easily built locations. To provide some penalty for violations, these radius restrictions should include a clause stating that a shopping center landlord gets percentage rent from any sales at units in other malls that are operating in violation of the radius restriction—the penalty may escalate up to a landlord's right to terminate the lease for such a violation.

CO-TENANCY

A co-tenancy clause stipulates that the tenant's obligations are contingent upon the presence of other tenants. The provisions might re-

quire the continued operation of one or more anchors, or the operation of specific retail units comprising a minimum number of square
feet or percentage of GLA. Similar retailers often like to have their
"friends" in the center with them and will often insist that a certain
number of named tenants be open and operating or the landlord
would suffer certain penalties, for example, reduced rent. Co-tenancy
provisions should include language that specifies whether the landlord can substitute one store for another and clear language explain-
ing that a temporary closure for renovation or remodeling is not
to be treated as a trigger for enforcing this clause. Sometimes, co-
tenancy clauses can be designed to expire after a set period of time,
giving the retailer time to establish its presence, and giving the landlord some relief from the requirements in time. Extensive co-tenancy
is very dangerous to the landlord. There are situations where a specific tenant named as a co-tenant went out of business and the landlord had no ability to substitute. This allowed other tenants to go on
a percentage-of-sales gross rent for the remainder of the term. With
the potential for stores to fail, the landlord must have a list of acceptable substitutes and alternatives. Reasonableness is a key word in any
co-tenancy clause if litigation occurs.

DEFAULT

If a tenant or landlord fails to fulfill the requirements of the lease,
then that party is considered in default. Shopping center leases tend
to emphasize tenant defaults, since the landlord wants to sustain un-
interrupted cash flow. Defaulting can result in lease termination, a financial assessment or some other kind of penalty. Grace periods may
be granted to allow elimination of the default, such as compliance
with the lease. Grace periods for monetary remedies tend to be
shorter than for nonmonetary penalties, since the latter have greater
effect on overall shopping center operation and profitability. To be effective, the lease must specify possible events of default and possible
remedies. Some possible events of default are:

- Nonpayment of base rent or percentage rent
- Tenant bankruptcy or insolvency
- Vacating or abandoning the store premises
- Seizure of the store by law enforcement
- Failure to open or remain open as per lease terms
- Breach of other agreements, covenants or conditions of the lease

HOURS

The lease specifies the hours during which the store must operate (e.g., 10:00 A.M. to 10:00 P.M. Monday through Saturday, and noon to 5:00 P.M. on Sunday). Universal store operating hours are an important part of meeting shoppers' expectations. Hours clauses seem to be especially important in small centers, lifestyle centers and for the boutique-style stores whose operators might be reluctant to keep evening hours, for example. These clauses will also specify operating hours during the holiday season, which tend to be longer than during the rest of the year. A typical clause specifying operating hours is shown in Figure 5, below.

Figure 5

CONTINUOUS OPERATION

Except when, and to the extent that, the demised premises may be untenantable by reason of damage by fire or other casualty, tenant shall: (a) continuously and uninterruptedly use, occupy, operate and conduct its business in the entire demised premises using its best efforts to produce the maximum volume of gross sales and to help establish and maintain a high reputation for the whole shopping center, (b) unless prohibited by law or required by landlord to close, open for business each day (except Sundays) at 10:00 A.M. at the latest and remain open for business until 10:00 P.M. at the earliest and further hours as may be designated by landlord from time to time, (c) open for business on Sundays from 10:00 A.M. until 6:00 P.M. or at such other hours as landlord shall designate from time to time, and (d) open for business on holidays at times as landlord shall designate from time to time. Notwithstanding the foregoing, if tenant's business is controlled by governmental regulations, the hours of operation prescribed by such governmental regulations shall apply. Tenant shall keep its store fully staffed continuously, and fully stocked with saleable seasonal merchandise of quality and otherwise appropriate to the permitted uses. Failure on tenant's part to comply with this section shall result in an assessment of five hundred and no/100 dollars ($500.00) per day.

TENANT IMPROVEMENTS AND THEIR PAYMENT

Tenant improvements, tenant allowances and tenant improvement allowances are really the same thing; different markets use the terms differently and there can be slight variations. All mean some form of compensation to the tenant. Depending on how the accounting is handled, funds spent for the preparation of a space to be occupied can be a tenant improvement. Adding new HVAC or carpet and paint all are expenses that fall into that category. The other portion of the definition relates to actual cash that is given to the tenant to assist with the building of the store. In today's leasing market, it is fairly common for a tenant to ask for a capital contribution from the landlord to open their store. The landlord, hopefully, has calculated a rental rate without any capital and another with capital so that there is an incremental return built into the funds given to the tenant. The payment of those funds has become more difficult recently, as tenants are demanding a certain portion of the money before construction in some cases. Usually the agreed amount is split between levels of completion of the work. Often, 50 percent of the funds are paid when 50 percent of the work is complete as verified by management. Another clause regarding the completion stage might specify that 40 percent is payable when the store is complete and the final 10 percent when the landlord has made a final approval, certificate of occupancy is issued, all lien waivers are completed and the tenant has commenced rental payment. Of course, as in any lease clause, there are many variations and it has become another topic of negotiation.

When any tenant allowance or improvement funds are negotiated, the landlord should maintain responsible control over their use. The negotiation should include landlord approval of the plans for the space, inspections as needed and other means to allow the landlord to know that the funds are used to improve the space and not for merchandise or other items. There are certainly tenants who may not grant that oversight and others who may be spending tenant improvement dollars for items the landlord would not usually approve, but that is all part of the negotiation.

LEGAL

Legal issues are a large part of any discussion of leases—after all, the lease is a legal document. Good legal counsel is essential in the negotiation of the lease agreement. The landlord usually prefers to have a standard lease agreement that is used for all the tenants in the shopping center. This aids management in finding specific clauses or concerns within the document. Some tenants prefer their own document, usually for the same reason.

The landlord will count on the legal team to protect his or her basic rights in the creation of the original lease document; the legal team should be consulted when changes are made during the process of the negotiation. Often, the legal team is not directly involved with the business terms of the lease (i.e., rental rate or charges), but it will certainly have an opinion on how those clauses are structured.

Legal representation should be well versed in local, regional and state law to create a sound lease document.

RECIPROCAL EASEMENT AGREEMENT (REA)

An REA is an agreement, typically between an anchor store or stores and a shopping center landlord, that grants each party certain rights to use of their respective properties. These uses may include parking, access, signage and others. Anchors will seek significant input and control over the rights and obligations granted or restricted under an REA. The leasing agent should determine if a center has an REA, become familiar with its terms and abide by them.

PERCENTAGE RENT

Percentage rent is often called overage rent. Sometimes a lease is based on a percentage of gross sales to determine the total rental paid—such an arrangement would allow the tenant to pay a simple percentage of total sales, for example, sales of $100,000 with a 10 percent rate would result in a gross rent of $10,000.

Usually, however, percentage rent (or overage rent) refers to the rental collected from a retailer for sales beyond a certain level referred to as the "breakpoint." The theory behind the idea for percentage rent comes from the early days of the industry. Retailers negotiated a percentage rent factor based on the type of business they were in. Higher margin-of-profit stores usually had higher percentages and vice versa. A jewelry store might have a percentage factor near 10 percent while a grocery store might be at 4–5 percent. The amount of base rent (not including CAM or other charges) for the year was divided by the percentage factor to create a breakpoint. The breakpoint was the amount of sales where the retailer was deemed to be "making money"—all the bills were being paid and the profit had begun. The landlord felt that the retailer should pay some portion of those profits to him, as the success of the retailer was likely due to the location in the shopping center. The percentage factor mentioned above was the factor used to determine how much was owed the landlord. If a jewelry store had a $100,000 annual rent with a 10-percent factor, the breakpoint would be $1,000,000 and when sales reached $1,000,001, the landlord would receive an extra 10 cents. As sales rose above the breakpoint, so did the amount of the percentage rent collected.

ANNUAL RENT / PERCENTAGE RENT FACTOR = BREAKPOINT
GROSS SALES – BREAKPOINT ¥ PERCENTAGE RENT
FACTOR = LL PERCENTAGE RENT

The definition of what is and is not a part of gross sales comes from the lease clause but, typically, the landlord may try to restrict any deduction for uncollected or uncollectible credit accounts or other losses. Other items such as sales taxes, excise taxes and exchanges/refunds of merchandise are usually not included in gross sales. Sales of store merchandise over the Internet or from catalogs is an area for negotiation—the customer is not on-site, but the sales may come through the on-site computer of the retailer. National chains with extensive internet operations will not generally agree to such clauses, but a smaller, more regional tenant may. A typical lease clause on percentage rent is shown in Figure 6 below.

Figure 6

PERCENTAGE RENT

The term "gross sales" shall mean the total amount in dollars of the actual sales price, whether for cash, on credit or both, of all sales of merchandise and services and all other receipts of business conducted in or from the demised premises, including all mail or telephone orders received or filled at the demises premises, all deposits not refunded to purchases, orders taken, although said orders may be filled elsewhere, and sales by any sublessee, concessionaire or licensee or otherwise in said demised premises. No deduction shall be allowed for uncollected or uncollectible credit accounts. Gross sales shall not include: sales or excise tax, nor the exchange of merchandise.

"FAVORED-NATIONS" CLAUSE

Borrowed from the field of international trade, this type of clause states that any provision or consideration given to another store must also be given to the tenant signing the lease in which the favored-nations clause appears. These clauses are less popular now than in years past, since they place the landlord at a serious disadvantage.

KICKOUTS

These clauses grant the tenant the right to leave a shopping center if sales do not reach a figure agreed upon by the landlord and tenant. Retailers want this figure to be low; landlords want this figure to be high. These clauses are becoming increasingly popular, particularly with very desirable tenants. When they do exist, they should be accompanied by clauses that say that the tenant has to reimburse the landlord for the cost of any buildouts and improvements made by the landlord for the tenant. There may be a negotiated settlement fee for the tenant leaving, or the fee may reflect the unamortized portion of the expenses the landlord incurred to get the tenant open, which may include tenant improvements, brokerage commissions, etc. In very strong shopping centers, the landlord can insert a reciprocal clause for the landlord to have the right to kick out a tenant who is not performing at sales levels needed by the landlord.

Summary

Many other types of clauses can be part of the lease, and each clause is under scrutiny during every lease negotiation. The goal is to maintain a lease agreement as close as possible to the landlord's original intentions. When the inevitable changes occur, they need to be factored into the final decision to proceed with a lease agreement.

In the end, the lease is the tool that the shopping center management team uses to run the shopping center. The lease determines everything from the business decisions on the correct charges for rent and CAM through insurance decisions to who is responsible for problems and what happens when the tenant leaves the shopping center.

A thorough knowledge and understanding of each and every lease at the center will improve the efficiency of operations, minimize legal battles and likely improve tenant relationships.

6 | Leasing from a Retailer's Perspective

Craig B. Sorrels

Understanding the Retailer

RETAIL FUNDAMENTALS

From the retailer's perspective, leasing is about sales. All occupancy costs—base rent, percentage rent, improvements, etc.—are evaluated on the sales volume that can be generated at a given location.

Each type of retailer, however, looks at the sales and costs from a different viewpoint—the merchandise, the price points, how often the inventory will turn. A high-end jeweler, for example, will judge lease components somewhat differently from a discount jeweler: they will each have different expectations about profitability of the leased space. So will the different types of retailers: a jewelry store might be quite satisfied to have the inventory turn over once per year, but a jeans store would feel otherwise.

The retailer needs to do some research before setting these expectations of sales versus expense. ICSC and other industry sources publish this kind of data for the various merchandise categories. This data can help retailers figure out what kind of rent demands can be expected and whether a deal offer is in line with industry norms.

Too often, retailers' sales expectations are too high, and as a result they accept deals whose occupancy costs are too high to meet unless their sales dreams are achieved. The retailer ought to take a conservative approach—perhaps basing occupancy costs on a lower projection of sales until they have more stores to make sure projections are correct. If, in the end, those dreamed-of sales figures are achieved, the retailer will be happy and the landlord will benefit through percentage rent.

Retailers should also keep the conservative approach in mind when designing their stores. Too much expense in design and construction may exceed the owner's tenant improvement allowance, and the store will be at a disadvantage literally before it opens.

Retailer Ownership and Categories

Most smaller tenants are privately held and owned. Most national and retail tenants are publicly traded companies.

RETAIL CATEGORIES

To understand leasing from the retailer's perspective, one should recognize the six large categories of retailers:

1. *Traditional general merchandise retailers.* These are the older department store chains: Macy's, Dillard's, Federated Stores.
2. *Contemporary general merchandise retailers.* This category includes a range of store types, price points and other factors. There are the smaller-footprint non-mall department store chains such as TJ Maxx, Kohl's and Marshalls, but also specialty department store chains such as Neiman Marcus, Saks and Nordstrom. Mass merchandisers such as Wal-Mart and Target fit in this category as well. Category specialists also fit here—Barnes & Noble, DSW Shoes, wholesale clubs, off-price factory outlet stores, catalogue showrooms and (mostly in Europe) hypermarkets.
3. *Food retailers.* This category includes a variety of distribution approaches. Wal-Mart, Tom Thumb and Target are all food retailers.
4. *Non-store retailers.* Internet retailers and some airport retailers are included here, although some have stores as well.
5. *Service retailers.* This group includes another broad range of merchandise, from muffler shops and gas stations to food service operations and dry cleaners.
6. *Entertainment/restaurant retailers.* This category includes the obvious—sit-down restaurants, movie theaters, etc.—but also stores with a strong entertainment component such as The Disney Store.

These are the retail formats most generally found in the United States. Europe, however, adds one more: the hypermarket, a major retail format that has not found a place in the United States. Hyper-markets are huge operations where shoppers can buy practically any-thing under the sun: soft goods, hard goods, groceries—and even car dealerships.

Understanding the Lease

The retailer sees the lease from a different perspective than the owner. The retailer, for example, will look at the term of the lease and think, "How long will it take me to amortize a store?" or "How long will it take to get profitable?"

The key is that retailers know (if they make the projections) that the store can be profitable. The lease should be reviewed by attorneys with lease experience before the retailer signs the document.

RENT STRUCTURE/TERM

The owner's goal, of course, rests with percentage rent. Many retail-ers still fail to understand the concept of percentage rent and why it works as a motivator for both owner and tenant. If the tenant can exceed the breakpoint (the point at which rent due from a specific percentage of sales equals the minimum rent), in most cases the store will be successful and profitable. The landlord should be happy as well.

ESCALATIONS AND USE CLAUSES

Two other types of lease clauses—escalation and use clauses—can help a retailer evaluate the true degree of the owner's interest in his or her store. An escalation is the landlord's demand for a fixed raise in rent. Success in this demand often depends on the strength of the tenant and how in-demand the retailer is. Use clauses define in the lease the product and scope of business of the retailer.

Other clauses also protect the landlord's interests. Radius restric-tions allow a landlord to limit how many stores a retailer can have in a certain area, usually defined by miles. A clause defining market-ing charges will reimburse the landlord for common area mainte-nance (CAM) charges, taxes, marketing costs and utilities.

CO-TENANCY, CAM AND OWNER'S CONTRIBUTIONS

The retailer will closely examine the co-tenancy clauses in the lease. The retailer will use these to be located near desirable tenants and those in the same category. A dress shop will want to be near an accessories store, for example, and not next to a game store, since there would be little cross-shopping.

A common area restriction clause is sought by most retailers, since it protects them against a kiosk being located near the storefront. This clause also makes sure the same type of product is not sold in the kiosk.

Also, the landlord can offer a tenant an owner's contribution—a cash allowance or even free rent—as an enticement to leasing space.

The Retailer's Environment

Like the owner/developer, the retailer also has management.

- Strategic management is the role of the president/CEO and his or her executive team. This group has overall responsibility for the company's performance.
- Merchandising management is concerned with the chain's product line, marketing and related issues. This group is also involved with vendor relationships and company inventory.
- Store management focuses, obviously, on where the merchandise is sold.
- Marketing directs branding, communication, events and customer relations.
- Administrative management is concerned with accounting, human resources, and so on.

Some companies also have other management units:

- Real estate management, which oversees planning and construction for freestanding stores.
- Non-store retailing, which concerns itself with catalog and online retailing.

Fundamentals of Retail Merchandising

CHANNELS OF DISTRIBUTION

Within the retail industry, companies have a variety of distribution channels for products. Some companies are said to be vertically integrated—that is, they manufacture the products, they transport it to the store and company personnel sell the products.

Some retailers sell to other retailers—these are not vertically integrated, since another retail company is involved at some point in the process, most likely the actual sale of the product to the customer. Department stores, for example, are not vertically integrated. They do not manufacture most of the items they sell—they buy them from other manufacturing companies.

RETAIL MATH

In many respects, the retailers' math comes down to the profit-and-loss statement (also known as the operating statement), which measures the results of operations. It shows revenues and expenses by specific categories and reports profit or loss for the current accounting period, which could be a month, a quarter or a year. Due to the seasonality of the shopping center and retail industries, results can be easily distorted when only a partial year is being reviewed.

Other terms of retail math are helpful to know:

- *Markup*—the difference in the retail selling price of the merchandise and the cost of the merchandise to the retailer.
- *Markdown*—a reduction in the retail selling price of the merchandise, primarily for clearance, special sales events or to meet competition.
- *Average inventory*—an average of the stock on hand at representative dates throughout the season or year.
- *Stock turnover*—the degree of balance between a retailer's inventory/sales and the speed with which its merchandise moves into and out of a department or store.
- *Gross margin*—the difference between the sales and the total cost of the merchandise sold.

COMMUNICATION

Finally, a retailer's perspective on leasing recognizes the value of communication between retailer and landlord. Clarity in lease clauses is essential to a deal that works to the benefit of both parties. Tenant design and construction are, at their root, communication activities. Owner-store relationships are also based on communication—and a landlord's representatives spend time well by sharing a cup of coffee with their store managers and asking about their issues. By doing so, both can be successful.

Communication between leasing agents relies on mutual respect. Phone calls should be returned promptly. Both parties should quickly deliver both the good news and any bad news. Mutual respect results in easier lease negotiations for the short term. In the long term, it results in relationships from which future lease deals can be completed.

7 | Specialty Leasing Strategies

Camilla L. Basse

Program Development

Specialty leasing is principally the leasing of space in the common areas of the shopping center, although it may apply to other areas of the mall as well. Specialty leasing can be thought of as the art of coming up with new and creative ways of driving income and maximizing occupancy.

One sees kiosks and carts throughout the center—those are the major part of specialty leasing. But many properties also find in-line space vacant from time to time, and these can be leased on a specialty basis, too.

OWNER EXPECTATIONS

Looking back to the 1980s, one would not find those kiosks and carts in the common area, which was typically devoted to benches, plants and trash receptacles. Visionary landlords, however, saw those areas as space. To a developer, space means income. So they started adding what were originally called pushcarts—later shortened to "carts"—which began to evolve as their own leasing category.

Kiosks evolved soon after. Kiosks, while also located in the common area of the center, are fully built structures that contain the salespeople and cash register in the interior of the kiosk. Merchandise is displayed on counters or tables on the exterior. Pretty soon, the carts and kiosks were commonplace, with specifically designated locations throughout the mall, and even lease lines or borders.

Income vs. Image. To make kiosks and carts work, they cannot violate the integrity of the common area. The units themselves should not interrupt the flow of traffic. They should not restrict entry to an in-line store or the shoppers' view of in-line stores. They should not obstruct views of upper floors, store-related signage or other visually significant objects. They should reflect restrictions in other stores' use clauses by not duplicating merchandise. In short, carts and kiosks should always add to the shopping experience without detracting from the success of more permanent tenants.

Specialty leasing also includes short-term leasing. The owner may have a lag of 2, 3 or more months before a new tenant can enter an in-line space. During that time, if the new tenant's lease allows it, the owner can lease the vacant space to a temporary tenant.

Investment vs. Expense. There are very few expenses in specialty leasing—one reason why it is so attractive to landlords. The largest initial expense is the retail merchandising units (RMUs), which are the carts or pushcarts. These are bought by the owner, to guarantee that their look, size and other components are consistent throughout the mall. Some RMUs are actually grocery carts—each landlord examines whether that option is appropriate for the center's image.

Some RMUs have become very sophisticated over the years, and pricing can range as high as $30,000 per unit. It is not unusual to find as many as 40 to 50 RMUs in a superregional mall or realize a 100 percent return on the purchase investment within 6 to 12 months.

WHO IS INVOLVED

Who gets involved in a specialty leasing program? Obviously, the tenant is involved. From the owner's side, there is usually a specialty leasing rep, as well as the general manager, the operations manager, the on-site accountant and the manager's administrative assistant. At the regional level, someone with a title like group vice president would also be engaged.

Nationally, a company may have a group or committee that does leasing deals with national cart retailers, including those that just come in at holidays. These retailers go into the large majority of regional malls around the country, and it is more efficient for the deals to be done between the parent companies.

Landlords may or may not own the larger structures, the kiosks. These structures can range in size from 8 square feet to 20 square feet, with many options between. Kiosks are more expensive than carts, easily exceeding $40,000. It is not unusual to generate double the purchase price in each year's sales.

Some developers may own a few kiosks that are leased to start-ups or mom-and-pop stores that could succeed in a kiosk if only they were spared the purchase of the structure itself.

CREATING A STRATEGIC PLAN

An owner needs to have a strategic plan for the specialty leasing program. The strategic plan will consist of three components: inventory, restrictions and revenue streams.

Inventory means determining which types of space can be used for specialty leasing, especially whether vacant in-line space will be used or not. The owner will also need to assess how much space is available for specialty leasing, and where it is.

Restrictions mean lease restriction: Does any tenant's lease prohibit anything in the common area within x feet of the store? When such restrictions exist, a common distance is 100 feet. Nowadays, even the carts and kiosks are asking for lease restrictions—they want to keep other carts at a distance. Sometimes owners and cart retailers can reach a gentleman's agreement to bend the lease restrictions if, for example, the merchandise on the two carts is completely different. Leasing reps find it helpful to keep a list of all these restrictions on hand, perhaps in a notebook, since an answer is often needed quickly. A copy of the list should also be kept in the mall office, since cart retailers may just walk in the door and want to do a deal.

The owner will want to assess revenue streams as part of the strategic plan. The revenue stream for specialty leasing is year-round, and typically about 40 percent of that revenue stream is in the fourth calendar quarter.

Program Administration

Administering the specialty leasing program can be defined as deal documentation and operating controls.

DEAL DOCUMENTATION

In documenting the deal, the owner will choose between a lease and a license. Generally, a lease will be chosen for occupancy of more than 1 year. A license is usually used for a shorter period of time. Licenses have been granted for as little as 2 hours' occupancy. The owner and

Figure 1

Specialty Retail
SAMPLE EXPENSE BUDGET
Start – Up
<u>Planning Sheet</u>

Inventory Expense:
Merchandise _____
Shipping _____
Storage _____

Rent Expense:
Base Rent _____
Overage _____
CAM Fees _____
Security Deposits _____

Visual Merchandising Expense:
Displays _____
Supplies _____
Services _____
Set – Up _____

Security Expense:
Locks _____
Alarms _____

Equipment Expense:
Cash Register _____
Credit Card Machine _____
Telephone _____
Other _____

Administrative Expense:
Bank Fees (night deposit fees, etc)
_____

Credit Card Fees (typical 2.4% of all CC sales)
_____

Insurance _____
Business License _____
Re-sale Certificate _____
Services (accountant) _____
Mileage _____

Payroll Expense:
Wages _____
Payroll Taxes _____
Bonus/Incentives _____
Classifieds _____

Other Expenses:
Advertising _____
Storage _____

TOTAL EXPENSES:

_____

specialty leasing rep should try to assess what would be a reasonable period of time to test a temporary tenant's viability. Most cannot hit their stride in 1 month—a 3-month trial would give a better indication. Longer than 6 months, on the other hand, might be too long for the owner to risk the space with a brand-new retailer.

Permanent leases will include addendums and exhibits, but these items are rarely included in licenses with small or local retailers. Some

Figure 2

SAMPLE
TEMPORARY LICENSE AGREEMENT

SECTION I

Date Prepared: *date written & submitted for approval*	**Term:** *# of months & days (C.D. through T.E.D.) up to 1 year*	**Commencement Date:** *open/ rent start date*	**Term End Date:** *expiration*
Termination Date: *Not used*	**Serial Number:** *Not used*		
Licensee's Legal Name *Person's legal name. If they want to use corporate name here, use "person's legal name and corporate name"*		**Shopping Center/Licensor**	
Licensee's Trade Name (DBA) *Store name*			
Licensee's Principal Address *Home or business address, NOT mall address. If P.O. Box, also include physical address.*			
Licensee's Phone Number *Contact's phone # (not store #)*		**Use Clause*** *"For the sale, at retail, of… and for no other purpose whatsoever." If not selling, then "For the display" or "For storage" etc.*	
Licensee's Principal Contact(s) *All contact names*			
Space ID *In-line: space # from Lease Plan* **Common:** *"Common Area # ____"*	**Square Feet** *In-line: sf+/- from Lease Plan* **Common:** *"32+/- Standard RMU" or actual sf if on own unit*	**Electricity** *In-line: total electricity charges for term* **Common:** *delete if no electricity charges*	
Base Fee *Total rent for term, including Advanced Fee*	**SLR** *Total common area charges for term or "N/A"*	**Marketing** *Total marketing charges for term or "N/A"*	**Advanced Fee** *$500.00 or "N/A" (charge to hold space- deducted from 1st month's rent)*

SECTION II

Fee Due Period/Month	Fee & Other Charges	Percent	Percent Base	Date Percent Due
Advanced Fee/due upon execution	$500.00 *Delete line if no Advanced Fee charged*			
1st of month	*Total due for month (SLC/SLI, SLR, Marketing, Electricity)* **see examples below**	*In-line:* 10% *Common:* 15%	*In-line: Monthly Base Fee / 10%* *Common: Monthly Base Fee / 15%*	*5th of next month*
July 1, 2003 **EXAMPLE: IN-LINE**	*$1,500.00 ($1,233 Base Fee, $61 SLR, $99 Marketing, $107 Electricity)*	*10%*	*$12,330.00*	*August 5, 2003*
August 1, 2003 **EXAMPLE: COMMON**	*$1,000.00 ($900 Base Fee, $36 CAM, $64 Marketing)*	*15%*	*$6,000.00*	*September 5, 2003*

NOTES ON SECTION II
- *If 1st month is not full month, Fee Due Period/Month will be Commencement Date and charges should be prorated based on # of days open. Prorated amounts for each charge should be included in totals in Section I and Percent Base (breakpoint) should be prorated.*
- *In 1st month's breakpoint, include the Advanced Fee amount with Base Fee to figure breakpoint.*
- *License Agreement template has 12 months worth of dates filled in. If License Agreement is for less than 1 year, delete the unused dates (you don't need to delete the rows in the table).*
- *If Gross Sales report date is changed from the 5th of the following month, also change the Date Percent Due.*
- *SLR charge usually 5% of Base Fee. Marketing charge usually 8% of Base Fee. You can round these off, but don't let them exceed 5% and 8%.*
- *If the total due for a month (and the breakdown of charges) is the same for more than 1 month, only the 1st entry for that amount needs to broken down by charge.*
- *Include a Percent and Percent Base for every month that Percent Fee will be calculated.*

NOTES ON ENTIRE LICENSE AGREEMENT
- *DO NOT delete anything. If part of the Agreement does not apply, strikethrough that language and change the font color to red.*
- *If language is added to the body of the Agreement, bold that language and change the font color to red.*
- *If you need to add language that does not fit with any numbered paragraph, add a paragraph 19.*

(continued)

_____ ("Licensor") hereby grants to *insert legal name here* ("Licensee") a non-exclusive, non-transferable, revocable and temporary license to sell, at retail as specifically described in Section I herein at _____ ("The Shopping Center") within a location ("premises") determinable and subject to change, at the direction of the Shopping Center Manager for the period ("the term") as specifically described in Section I herein.

LICENSOR AND LICENSEE ACKNOWLEDGE AND HEREBY AGREE THAT THIS TEMPORARY LICENSE AGREEMENT DOES NOT AND SHALL NOT, IN ANY WAY, CREATE THE RELATIONSHIP OF LANDLORD/TENANT BETWEEN LICENSOR AND LICENSEE AND BOTH PARTIES AGREE THAT NO TENANCY OF ANY KIND IS IMPLIED OR CREATED BY THIS DOCUMENT.

1. BASIC FEE Licensee shall pay fee and other charges ("Fee") as specifically described in Section II herein to Licensor. Fee and other charges are due and payable without any offset or deduction, in advance, without notice or invoice from Licensor, for each one month period on the 1st day of each said month, unless otherwise specifically stated in Section II herein.

2. PERCENTAGE FEE If Gross Sales (as hereinafter defined) shall be greater than the Percent Base as specifically described in Section II herein, then Licensee shall pay to Licensor, as additional fee, Percentage Fee ("Percentage Fee") as specifically described in Section II herein on the amount of Gross Sales in excess of the Percent Base on or before the fifth day following the period month.
Strikethrough this paragraph if no Percentage Fee calculation.

3. PAYMENT Payment of Fee, Percentage Fee and any other sums due herein shall be made in certified check, cashiers check, bank money order, or personal check (at Licensor's option) only, payable to Colonial Properties and shall be delivered to the Shopping Center Management Office when due. Licensee shall pay to Licensor a Fifty Dollar ($50) fee for all checks returned from the bank as non-sufficient funds.

4. LATE FEES If Licensee fails to make any payment of Fee, Percentage Fee or any other sums due herein, Licensee shall pay to Licensor a late fee of $25.00 per day for each day from the 10th day following the due date thereof until such sums are paid.

5. GROSS RECEIPTS DEFINED As used herein the term "Gross Sales" shall mean all revenues, income and compensation received by Licensee as a result of its business at the Shopping Center including, the actual price of all goods and merchandise sold, leased or licensed and the charges for all services performed by Licensee or otherwise from all business conducted at or from the Shopping Center, whether made for cash, by check, credit or otherwise, without reserve or deduction for inability or failure to collect the same. Licensor will deliver to the Shopping Center Management Office a statement of Gross Sales for the preceding period/month on or before the fifth day following the preceding period/month.
Strikethrough this paragraph if no Percentage Fee calculation.

6. LICENSEE'S RECORDS For the purpose of permitting verification by Licensor of any Gross Sales reports due under this agreement, Licensee will keep and preserve for at least six months after the termination of this agreement original or duplicate books and records which shall disclose all information required to determine any percentages due thereon. In addition, Licensee shall make available within 48 hours said duplicate books and records to Licensor upon demand from Licensor. If such audit shall disclose a deficiency in the payment of Percentage Fee, then such deficiency shall become immediately due and payable. In addition, if Licensee's statement shall be found to have understated Gross Sales by two percent (2%) or more, then Licensee shall pay Licensor's entire reasonable audit and other costs and expenses related thereto.
Strikethrough this paragraph if no Percentage Fee calculation.

7. ADVANCE FEE Licensee shall deliver to Licensor, together herewith, an advance fee payment ("Advance Fee") of $500.00, which shall be held by Licensor to secure performance and opening for business by Licensee. So long as Licensee shall comply with all pre-opening requirements and shall open for business as stipulated, said Advance Fee shall be applied to the first month's fee obligation, failing which the Advance Fee shall be automatically forfeited by Licensee (and become the property of Licensor).
Strikethrough this paragraph if no Advanced Fee.

8. RULES & REGULATIONS Licensee shall abide by and comply with all rules and regulations being found attached to this agreement as **Exhibit A**. Licensee's failure to comply with rules and regulations as set forth in said exhibit will constitute a $15.00 per day fine until compliance is restored as well as be construed by Licensor as an event of default under this agreement.

(continued)

national specialty retailers, however, do have a standard addendum that is attached to the license or lease.

The license or lease will also include a kickout agreement (also known as a "termination agreement"), meaning that the landlord can, with or without cause, revoke the license agreement and move or evict the cart tenant, usually on 24 hours' notice. While this is sometimes used to rid the mall of an annoying or underproducing

9. PERMITS Licensee shall, at its sole cost and expense and prior to the commencement of any occupancy under this License Agreement, obtain all permits or licenses required by any governmental authority for the operation of Licensee's particular type of business to be conducted on the premises.

10. HOLD HARMLESS Licensee hereby assumes liability for and shall indemnify and hold harmless Licensor, the Shopping Center licensees, the owners and ground lessees of the real estate comprising the Shopping Center and their respective shareholders, officers, directors, employees, customers and invitees (all of the foregoing being hereinafter collectively referred to as the "Indemnitees") from and against any and all liability, loss, cost, damage or expense (including, without limitation, costs of litigation and attorneys' fees) that any of the Indemnitees shall ever suffer or incur in connection with loss of life, bodily and/or personal injury, or damage to property arising out of or from the use or occupancy by the Licensee of the premises, or any part thereof, or any other part of the Shopping Center, or occasioned wholly or in part by any act or omission of Licensee, or its dealers, employees, promoters, agents, guests, invitees or contractors, or in any way relating to or arising out of any activity of the Licensee. The Licensee also agrees to release the Indemnities from any liability in regard to any loss, theft, burglary, robbery or damage to equipment, supplies, prizes, merchandise, exhibits or other property of the Licensee or any of its dealers, employees, promoters, agents, guests, invitees or contractors. Licensee also agrees to indemnify and hold the Indemnitees harmless from and against any and all liability, loss cost, damage or expense (including, without limitation, costs of litigation and attorney's fees) that any of the Indemnitees shall ever suffer or incur in connection with any claims arising out of the consumption, or existence in, on or about the Shopping Center, of any goods, products, consumables or merchandise sold or furnished by Licensee or its employees, promoters, agents or contractors.

11. WAIVER To the full extent permitted by law, Licensee hereby releases Licensor from any liability for damage to property of Licensee or any other person claiming through Licensee resulting from any accident or occurrence in or upon the premises or any other part of the Shopping Center.

12. INSURANCE Licensee will provide to the Licensor at least ten (10) days prior to commencement of the term of this License Agreement a certificate of insurance establishing that the Licensee carries insurance coverage with a reputable insurance company authorized to transact business in the State in which the Shopping Center is located, having coverages and limits as indicated below: (a) Comprehensive general liability and property damage insurance having limits of not less than $1,000,000 for bodily or personal injury to, death, or destruction of property. Said insurance shall include contractual liability coverage to insure Licensee's obligations hereunder; (b) Workmen's Compensation Insurance as required by the laws of the State where the Shopping Center is located. (c) Other _____(Specify). The aforementioned certificate shall establish that the insurance will be in full force and effect at the commencement of the term of this License Agreement and shall name the following as additional insured thereunder: _____ and shall provide that no such insurance may be canceled without at least ten (10) days notice to the Licensor.

13. LIENS Licensee agrees not to permit any mechanics' or material-men's lien to be filed against the premises by reason of any work, labor, services or materials performed at or furnished to the premises for Licensee or anyone occupying the premises under Licensee. Nothing in the License Agreement shall be construed as a consent on the part of the Licensor to subject the Licensor's estate in the premises to any lien liability under the lien laws of the State in which the Shopping Center is located. In the event any such mechanic's liens or material-men's lien are filed, Licensee shall discharge the same immediately and failure to do so shall constitute default under this agreement.

14. RELOCATION/TERMINATION Licensor may relocate Licensee or terminate this license agreement, with or without cause, at any time during the term of the agreement by giving Licensee not less than forty-eight (48) hours advance notice. Notification period commences on the date correspondence is post marked. Licensor may revoke this License Agreement at any time upon written notice for any default under this License Agreement. In the event of default, Licensee will quit and surrender premises immediately as described in section 18 hereunder.

15. USE/ASSIGNMENT/SUBLETTING Licensee shall use the premises only for the use specifically granted by this License Agreement and shall not sell any items or perform any services not specifically permitted hereby without Licensor's written consent, which may be withheld in Licensor's sole discretion. Licensee shall, at all times, comply with all laws, ordinances and restrictions affecting the Shopping Center and shall conduct its business at the Shopping Center in a manner so as not to create a nuisance or cause unreasonable distraction to the licensees of the Shopping Center and shall not interfere with the conduct of any licensee's business located in the Shopping Center. Licensee shall not voluntarily or by operation at law or otherwise, assign, transfer mortgage or otherwise encumber all or part of Licensees' interest in this license agreement or in the premises or sublet the whole or any part of the premises without first obtaining in each and every instance the prior written consent of the Licensor, which consent may be withheld in Licensor's sole discretion.

16. SUCCESSOR/ASSIGNS This License Agreement and the covenants and conditions herein contained shall inure to the benefit of and be binding upon Licensor, its successors and assigns and shall be binding upon Licensee, its successors and assigns and shall inure to the benefit of Licensee and only such assigns of Licensee to whom the assignment by Licensee has been consented by Licensor in accordance with the preceding paragraph of this license agreement.

(continued)

tenant, it is more often used when a new in-line tenant has a lease restriction that makes it impossible for the cart tenant to continue in that spot. These termination agreements are one-way: the landlord can evict the tenant on 24 hours' notice, but the tenant cannot leave voluntarily until the end of the lease or license period. In-line temporary tenants, of course, probably could not comply with 24 hours'

17. DEFAULT In the event of any failure of Licensee to pay any sums when due hereunder, or any failure to perform any other of the terms, conditions or covenants of this License Agreement to be observed or performed by Licensee or if Licensee shall become bankrupt or insolvent, or file any debtor proceedings, or take or have taken against Licensee in any court pursuant to any statute, either of the United States or any State, a petition in bankruptcy or insolvency or for reorganization or for the appointment of a receiver or trustee of all or a portion of Licensee's property, or if Licensee makes an assignment for the benefit of creditors, or petitions, or enters into an arrangement, or if Licensee shall cease conducting its business at the Premises or changes its use without Licensor's consent or shall abandon said premises, then Licensor, in addition to all other rights and remedies it may have at law and in equity, shall have the following remedies:

    a)   All sums due hereunder as specifically defined in Section 2 herein for the balance of the term as specifically described in Section 1 herein and all other sums and charges payable hereunder as fee or otherwise for the balance of the term or any part thereof, at the option of the Licensor, shall immediately upon notice become due and payable as if by the terms of this License Agreement they are payable in advance; and, Licensor may immediately proceed to distrain, collect, or bring action for said sums or such part thereof as being in arrears, or may file proof of claim in any bankruptcy or insolvency proceedings for such sums, or Licensor may institute any other proceedings whether similar to the foregoing or not, to enforce payment thereof.

    b)   Licensor, in addition to all other rights and remedies it may have, shall have the immediate right of reentry and may remove all persons and property from the premises and such property may be removed and stored in a public warehouse or elsewhere at the cost of and for the account of Licensee, all without notice or resort to legal process and without Licensor being deemed guilty of trespass, or becoming liable for any loss or damage which may be occasioned thereby.

    c)   Licensee agrees to pay on demand all expenses (including attorneys' fees and court costs) incurred by Licensor in enforcing any obligations of Licensee under this agreement.

18. END OF TERM At the expiration or sooner termination of the Term, Licensee shall (a) quit and surrender to Licensor the Premises in good order and condition, (b) remove all property of Licensee and (c) repair all damage to the Premises caused by such removal and restore the Premises to the condition in which it was prior to the installation of the items so removed. If the Licensee fails to surrender the premises to the Licensor upon the expiration or termination of this License Agreement in accordance with the terms herein then the Licensee shall pay, as liquidated damages to the Licensor an amount equal to twice the monthly rate as stated in Section II.

IN WITNESS WHEREOF, the parties hereto intending to be legally bound hereby executed this License Agreement as of *Fill in date when executing Agreement*, _____.

LICENSOR: **LICENSEE:**
                                               insert legal name here

By: _____   By:_____

Its:_____   Its:_____

---

notice, so these licenses usually specify notice of 15 days, 30 days or longer.

OPERATING CONTROLS

Check Logs. Operating controls comprise the other end of specialty leasing administration. The first operational control is the check log. This tracks whether the specialty retailer has paid rent on time. Usually, the license specifies that fines are collected on late rents starting on a specific day (e.g., the fifth day of the month if the rent was due on the first). The mall should determine appropriate methods of payments. Some malls will accept business checks. Others will only accept cashier's checks or money orders. Some mall offices are set up to accept credit card payments for rent—this way, the owner can sim-

Figure 3

SAMPLE

Specialty License Agreement

Licensee Contact: _____

Name: _____

Address: _____

_____

Phone: _____

This License Agreement is made this _____ day of _____ , 20 _____ , by and between _____ a _____ ("Licensor"), and _____ , a _____ ("Licensee"), having its principal offices at _____ .

In consideration of the mutual promises and obligations contained in this agreement, the parties agree as follows:

1. *Grant of License*. Licensor grants to Licensee a non-transferable, revocable License for the sole purpose of conducting the following business activities: _____

_____

(the "Business"), and for no other activity or purpose whatsoever in a location (the "Assigned Location") containing approximately_____ square feet, as more particularly described as _____ in that certain shopping center known as _____ ("Shopping Center") shown on Exhibit "A" attached hereto and made a part of this License.

   2. *Term*. Licensee shall be permitted to conduct the Business in the Assigned Location starting upon the earlier of (a) _____ or (b) the day Licensee actually commences conducting Business in the assigned location ("Commencement Date") and ending no later than _____ (the "Expiration Date"), unless this License is revoked earlier by Licensor. Licensor may revoke this License at will, and without cause, effective immediately upon personal delivery of written notice of revocation to Licensee or Licensee's employees or agents at the Assigned Location or by overnight delivery service to Licensee's address set forth above. This License shall terminate without further notice or action by Licensor upon delivery of such notice, and Licensee shall upon receipt of said notice vacate the assigned location and cease conducting business.

   3. *Trade Name*. Licensee shall conduct the Business under the trade name which Licensee represents it has a right to use and which shall not be changed without Licensor's approval.

   4. *Consideration*. Licensee shall pay Licensor for this License, without notice or demand, at _____ or such other location as Licensor may specify, by COMPANY check or cashier's check PAYABLE TO:_____ .

      (i)   Total Base License Fee_____

              Schedule of Payments _____

              The Base License Fee shall include operational fees.

      (ii)   Total Marketing Fund Fee _____

              Schedule of Payments _____

      (iii)   ____ % of all net sales and revenues in excess of $ _____ ("Percentage License Fee") is payable on the expiration date, or by the 10th following each month. For the purpose of this License, "net sales and revenues" shall mean all sales prices of goods and merchandise sold, leased or charged and the full charges for all services and all other receipts by Licensee within the Shopping Center, excluding sales tax.

Licensor _____

Licensee _____

(Continued)

(iv) $ _____ ("Visual Communication Fee") is included in your payment schedule and is payable on _____ .

The Base Rent Fee, Marketing Fund Fee, Percentage License Fee and Visual Communication Fee are collectively referred to herein as "Fees."

Irrespective of whether a Visual Communication Fee is charged by Licensor, Licensee shall follow the visual merchandising directives given to it by Licensor and may change the visual merchandising only in accordance with Licensor's request or approval from time to time. Any designs, concepts, layout sketches, props and other materials provided by or on behalf of Licensor in connection with visual merchandising shall remain the sole property of Licensor. All such materials shall be returned to Licensor at the expiration or termination of this license or upon Licensor's request. Licensor reserves the right to photograph Licensee's Assigned Location and to use photographs or other depictions of Licensee's Assigned Location in advertising, promotional and marketing materials.

Concurrent with Licensee's execution of this License, Licensee agrees to deposit with Licensor a sum equal to $ _____ (____% of the Minimum License Fee), which shall be applied to the Licensee's total Fees due. If Licensee does not commence conducting the Business in the Assigned Location with the public for any reason, including termination of this License by Licensor, on or before _____ , this deposit shall be forfeited by Licensee.

If Licensee shall fail to make any payment to Licensor when due, Licensee shall pay Licensor a late charge of $25.00 per day as liquidated damages, in addition to and not in lieu of Licensor's other remedies, for as long as the failure continues.

5. Licensee shall deliver to Licensor a monthly written statement of all net sales and revenues with sales verification, signed by Licensee. On the 10th following each calendar month, Licensee shall deliver the report to Licensor. If the term of this License is less than one month, Licensee shall deliver to Licensor a written statement of all net sales and revenues with sales verification signed by Licensee on the last day on which Licensee conducts the Business in the Assigned Location. If Licensee does not deliver the report on time, Licensee shall pay Licensor immediately upon request $50.00 as liquidated damages, in addition to and not in lieu of Licensor's other remedies.

6. Licensee shall prepare in accordance with generally accepted accounting practice and keep at its principal office address, set forth above, accurate books of account and records of its net sales and revenues. All of Licensee's books and records shall be subject to examination and audit by Licensor. If there is a deficiency in the Percentage License Fee payable to Licensor, Licensee shall immediately pay Licensor the additional Percentage License Fee owed Licensor and also pay the cost of the examination or audit.

7. Licensor shall not be liable to Licensee for damages or otherwise for any delay or cessation in the start of the Business. The Assigned Location may be relocated at any time by Licensor, and this License may be revoked with or without cause by Licensor, with no liability in either case to Licensor.

8. Licensee shall carry workers' compensation insurance in the statutory amount and employer's liability insurance in the amount of $100,000 per accident and disease for each employee with a $500,000 limit for disease. Licensee shall carry commercial general liability insurance which shall include contractual liability endorsements and shall have minimum limits of $500,000 for bodily injuries to or death of any number of persons as a result of any occurrence and $500,000 for property damage. All such insurance policies shall contain a provision that Licensor and Licensee shall be given a minimum of 20 days' written notice by the insurance company prior to cancellation, termination or change in such insurance. Licensee's policy or policies shall name Licensor, its parents, subsidiaries and affiliates and Licensee as additional insureds. Licensee shall deposit certificates showing such coverage with Licensor prior to the earlier of the commencement of any construction by Licensee anywhere in or around the Shopping Center or the Commencement Date. All such insurance carriers shall be rated A-VII or better by Best's and shall be authorized to do business in the state in which the Shopping Center is located.

9. Starting on the date Licensee first commences the Business under this License, Licensee shall indemnify and hold Licensor, its managers, directors, shareholders, partners, employees, agents, attorneys, contractors, parents, subsidiaries and affiliates harmless from and against any and all claims, actions, liens, demands, expenses and judgments for loss, damage or injury to property or persons resulting or occurring by reason of the Licensee's construction activities under this License, or in any way connected with the operation of the Business, or otherwise arising from this License or Licensee's activities hereunder, including all costs, expenses and attorney's fees. Licensee shall also indemnify Licensor for all legal or litigation costs, expenses and attorney's fees incurred by Licensor to enforce this indemnity.

10. Licensor shall not be responsible or liable for, and Licensee hereby expressly waives, any and all claims against Licensor for injury to persons or damage to Licensee's property, regardless of cause. Licensee's property located anywhere in the Shopping Center shall be there at Licensee's sole risk and expense. Licensor, its agents, independent contractors and employees shall not be liable for, and Licensee waives, all claims for loss or damage to Licensee's Business or damage to persons or property sustained by Licensee or any person claiming by, through or under Licensee resulting from any accident or occurrence anywhere in, on or about the Shopping Center, including, without limitation, claims for loss, theft or carnage resulting from (i) equipment or appurtenances becoming out of repair; (ii) injury done or occasioned by wind or weather; (iii) any defect in or failure to operate, for whatever reason, of any sprinkler, heat-

Licensor _____

Licensee _____

(Continued)

ply run the card on the due date to collect payment, rather than have to have payment handed to them by the tenant. The tenant should be informed of acceptable methods of rent payment, either in the license or before the license is signed.

ing or air-conditioning equipment, electric wiring or the installation thereof, gas, water or steam pipes, stairs, porches, railings or walks; (iv) broken glass; (v) the backing up of any sewer pipe or downspout; (vi) the bursting, leaking or running of any tank, tub, washstand, water closet, waste pipe, drain or other pipe; (vii) the escape of steam or water; (viii) water, snow or ice being upon or coming through the roof, skylight, trapdoor, stairs, doorways, windows, walks or any other place upon or near the Shopping Center; (ix) the falling of any fixture, plaster, tile, stucco or other material; (x) any act, omission or negligence of other licensees or any other persons or occupants of the Shopping Center or at adjoining or contiguous buildings, or owners of adjacent or contiguous property or the public, or the construction of any private, public or quasi-public work, or (xi) any other cause of any nature. To the maximum extent permitted by law, Licensee agrees to operate its Business within the Shopping Center and to use any area, part or portion of the Shopping Center to the extent permitted by this License at Licensee's own risk.

11. If Licensee (a) fails to perform any of the terms, conditions, or covenants of this License; (b) becomes bankrupt or insolvent, or files any debtor proceedings, or takes or has taken in any state or federal court a petition in bankruptcy or insolvency or for reorganization or for the appointment of a receiver or trustee of all or a portion of Licensee's property, or makes an assignment for the benefit of creditors, or petitions for or enters into an arrangement; (c) ceases or fails to operate its Business in the Assigned Location either temporarily or permanently, Licensor, besides having the right to immediately revoke this License without serving notice to Licensee, shall have the immediate right to remove Licensee and any persons claiming rights under Licensee and their property from the Shopping Center, to lock and bar Licensee and all persons claiming rights under Licensee from doing Business in the Shopping Center, and to pursue all other remedies available to Licensor at law and in equity, including but not limited to the recovery of all fees and other sums payable to Licensor under this License. All rights and remedies of Licensor herein or at law are cumulative.

12. Licensee shall not sell, assign, mortgage, pledge, sublicense, grant concessions or transfer this License or any interest therein, without Licensor's prior written approval, which may be withheld at Licensor's sole and absolute discretion.

13. Licensor shall have no personal liability with respect to this License. If a breach by Licensor occurs, Licensee shall be limited in any recovery solely to the equity of Licensor in the Shopping Center for the satisfaction of Licensee's remedies. As a specific condition of this License and in consideration for all of Licensor's covenants and performance herein, Licensee specifically agrees that this paragraph precludes Licensee from seeking any remedy for deficiency from Licensor's shareholders, partners, directors, officers, employees, agents, attorneys, contractors or any other person or entity.

14. Licensor is or may be a party to certain documents and agreements, as amended from time to time, with a mortgagee or beneficiary of Licensor, department stores, Shopping Center tenants and others. This License is subject and subordinate to all the provisions in those documents as they may be amended from time to time.

15. This License contains all the covenants, promises, agreements, conditions and understandings between Licensor and Licensee. This agreement supersedes all prior and contemporaneous statements, representations, agreements and understandings, including any such statements, representations, agreements and understandings Licensee may believe or later allege were made as inducements to enter into this agreement. There are no other agreements or binding representations, either oral or written, between Licensor and Licensee other than those set forth in this License.

16. If either Licensor or Licensee shall institute any action or proceeding against the other relating to the provisions of this License, then the unsuccessful party in the action or proceeding shall reimburse the successful party for all reasonable expenses and attorney's fees and disbursements incurred by the successful party.

17. It is understood and agreed that nothing contained in this License shall be considered as in any way constituting a partnership between Licensor and Licensee. Licensee agrees that it does not and shall not claim at any time any leasehold interest or other interest or estate of any kind or extent whatsoever in the Shopping Center or any part of the Shopping Center by virtue of the privileges granted under this License or by Licensee's activities under this License.

18. This License shall be governed by, construed, and enforced in accordance with the laws of the State of _____ .

19. Licensee's rights under this License shall be at all times subject to the rights of the Licensor in and to the Shopping Center. Said rights of Licensor include, without limitation, the right to enter the Assigned Location, to relocate the Assigned Location, and to terminate this License.

20. All costs and expenses (including permits or licenses) attributable to any construction by Licensee shall be borne solely by Licensee. Licensee shall not commence any construction in the Shopping Center prior to the execution of this License and without first obtaining Licensor's express written approval of the location and design. Design criteria for construction under this License are:

    a.   If the Assigned Location is a kiosk, the kiosk structure shall be limited to counter units with no overhead obstructions that inhibit the visibility of any tenant or business activity in the Shopping Center. Counter units shall not exceed 5'0" in height.

    b.   If the Assigned Location is a kiosk, the kiosk structure, if located in an open floor area, shall not be anchored into the floor or other part of the Shopping Center structure. Common area width of 10'0" minimum shall be maintained on all sides of the kiosk, subject to traffic flow.

    c.   If the Assigned Location is a kiosk, water service, special HVAC systems and fire sprinkler protection are not avail-

Licensor _____

Licensee _____

(Continued)

able. HVAC and fire protection systems shall be that which is provided to common areas in the Shopping Center.

d.   Design criteria for signage, construction, finish materials, special equipment and, if the Assigned Location is a kiosk, kiosk size shall be evaluated specifically for each Licensee. Licensee shall submit plans and specifications for Licensor's review and approval prior to commencement of construction. Pictures of existing Units should be provided.

e.   Licensee shall prepare its plans and perform all work to comply with governing statutes, ordinances, regulations, codes and insurance rating boards and apply for and obtain all necessary permits. Licensor's approval of Licensee's plans shall not relieve Licensee of its obligation to complete all work in accordance with the License, nor does Licensor's approval relieve Licensee from complying with laws, rules, regulations and requirements of local governing authorities, nor can Licensor's approval be relied upon by Licensee as verification of the sufficiency of the plans and specifications for any purpose or for compliance with any legal requirement. Certificates of occupancy and waivers of lien from Licensee's contractors, subcontractors and materialmen shall be filed with Licensor upon completion of work.

f.   If the Assigned Location is a kiosk, setup and teardown of kiosks must take place when the Shopping Center is not open for business, unless Licensor has otherwise agreed with Licensee in writing.

g.   All alterations, additions and improvements to the Assigned Location shall become upon completion the property of Licensor.

21. If there are any licenses, authorizations or permits required by any governmental agency or authority for the activity permitted under this License, Licensee shall be responsible for obtaining them. Licensee shall not conduct any unlawful activities in or upon any part of the Shopping Center. The consumption or sale of alcoholic beverages in, at or from the Assigned Location shall not be permitted.

22. This Section 22 shall apply only if the Assigned Location is not a kiosk or a cart. Licensor has caused or shall cause the necessary mains, conduits and other facilities to be provided to make available, as applicable, water, sewage disposal and electricity to the Assigned Location. Licensor has likewise caused or shall cause to be made available a heating and air-conditioning system. Licensee agrees to use and to pay for the use of such system in the manner prescribed by Licensor. Licensee agrees to use and to pay for all utilities used in the Assigned Location from and after the Commencement Date. If a separate meter is provided for utilities, it shall be at Licensee's expense. Licensor shall not be liable to Licensee for damages or otherwise if the utilities or heating and air-conditioning services are interrupted or terminated for any cause. If Licensor does not furnish or elects to discontinue furnishing any utilities or services, as the case may be, to the Assigned Location for any reason, Licensee shall obtain its own utilities or services, as the case may be, for or to the Assigned Location. If Licensee shall require natural gas for its normal operation, the natural gas utility service shall be available from the local gas company through the mains located in designated areas. All gas work beyond those points shall be arranged for by Licensee with the gas company, and such work shall be approved by Licensor and performed by Licensee at its sole expense. The parties understand that local gas supplies may be limited, and availability of sufficient gas to service the Assigned Location shall be Licensee's sole responsibility.

23. Licensee shall observe ail reasonable Operating Rules that Licensor may promulgate from time to time, including but not limited to the following:

a.   Licensee shall conduct the Business in a careful, safe and proper manner and shall keep the Assigned Location and the area around the Assigned Location in a clean and safe condition in accordance with this License, local ordinances and the directions of the manager of the Shopping Center and public safety officers.

b.   All signage located in, upon and about the Assigned Location must be approved by Licensor prior to installation or placement. All signs, placards, pennants and other advertising matter shall be prepared in a professional manner. Licensee shall display a sign depicting its approved trade name.

c.   Licensee shall not display merchandise on or outside the boundaries of the Assigned Location. The outside areas around and immediately adjoining the Assigned Location shall be kept clear at all times by Licensee, and Licensee shall not place or permit any obstructions, garbage, refuse, merchandise or displays in such areas.

d.   All loading and unloading of goods shall be done only at such times and in the areas and through the entrances designated for that purpose by Licensor.

e.   All garbage and refuse shall be kept in the kind of container specified by Licensor, and shall be placed and prepared for collection in the manner and at the times and places specified by Licensor.

f.   No loudspeakers, televisions, phonographs, radios, flashing lights, or other devices shall be used unless specifically approved by Licensor, which approval may be withdrawn at the sole and absolute discretion of Licensor upon personal delivery of written notice to Licensee or Licensee's employees or agents at the Assigned Location.

g.   There shall be no auction, fire, bankruptcy or selling-out (going-out-of-business) sale by Licensee.

h.   Licensee shall not carry on any trade or occupation or operate any instrument or equipment that emits any odor or causes any noise discernible to tenants or invitees of the Shopping Center or other licensees.

Licensor _____

Licensee _____

(Continued)

    i.   Licensee shall not distribute any handbills or other advertising matter in the Shopping Center or on automobiles parked in the parking areas of the Shopping Center.

    j.   Licensee and Licensee's employees shall not park their cars in those portions of the parking area designated for customer parking by Licensor. If Licensee or Licensee's employees park in portions of the parking area designated for customer parking, Licensor may, in addition to its other remedies, have the car removed at Licensee's expense.

    k.   Licensee and Licensee's employees and agents shall maintain a neat and appropriate appearance and dress whenever conducting Business in the Shopping Center. Licensee and Licensee's employees and agents shall not wear jeans or shorts while conducting Business in the Shopping Center.

24. Licensee shall at all times provide sufficient supervision and maintain adequate control of its employees, agents, guests and customers.

25. Licensee shall at the termination or revocation of this License remove its goods and effects, repair damage caused by such removal and peaceably yield up the Assigned Location clean and in good order, repair and condition. Personal property of Licensee not removed within forty-eight (48) hours shall become property of Licensor, at Licensor's option.

26. Licensee shall not harm the Shopping Center or any part thereof, commit waste, create a nuisance, or make any use of the Shopping Center that is offensive in Licensor's sole opinion, nor do any act that would, in Licensor's sole opinion, tend to injure the reputation of the Shopping Center. Licensee shall not make alterations or additions, nor permit the making of holes in the Shopping Center's walls, partitions, carts, ceilings or floors, nor permit the painting or placing of exterior signs, placards or other advertising media, banners, pennants, awnings, aerials, antennas, or the like in or about the Shopping Center without the prior written consent of Licensor. Licensee shall comply with all laws, ordinances, orders and regulations affecting the Business and this License. Any Licensee who damages or defaces any part of the Shopping Center will be assessed the cost of repairs plus a $50.00 administration fee.

27. Licensee has inspected the Assigned Location and accepts it "as is" with no representation or warranty by Licensor regarding the condition of the Assigned Location or its suitability for Licensee's Business. Licensor has no obligation to repair any part of the Assigned Location unless the obligation is set forth in this License.

28. Licensee shall operate the Business open to the public at all times designated by Licensor. Licensee shall operate the Business in a first-class manner and shall operate the Business uninterruptedly while this License is in effect.

29. Licensee shall not cause any hazardous material to be brought, stored, kept, used or discharged on or about any part of the Shopping Center.

30. Licensor may enter and/or inspect the Assigned Location at any time.

31. Licensee shall maintain, at its own cost and expense, the Assigned Location in good condition and make all necessary replacements and repairs to the Assigned Location. In addition to all other remedies of Licensor, if Licensee does not complete its obligations to repair and maintain the Assigned Location, or if Licensor, in the exercise of its sole discretion, determines that repair or replacement of any portion of the Assigned Location or the Shopping Center is necessary by reason of any act, omission or negligence of Licensee, its agents, employees, guests or customers, then, in any such event, Licensor may make, but shall not be obligated to make, such repairs without liability to Licensee for any loss or damage that may accrue to Licensee, its merchandise, fixtures, or other property or to Licensee's business by reason of such repair. Upon completion of any such repair, Licensee shall pay upon demand, as an additional Minimum License Fee, Licensor's costs for making the repairs together with Licensor's administrative costs related thereto, which amount shall equal 1.5 times the total cost of the repair.

32. Licensee agrees not to suffer any mechanic's lien to be filed against the Shopping Center by reason of any work, labor, services, or materials performed at or furnished to the Assigned Location, to Licensee, or to anyone claiming rights through or under Licensee. Nothing in this License shall be construed as a consent on the part of Licensor or subject Licensor's estate in the Shopping Center to any lien of liability under the lien laws of the state in which the Shopping Center is located.

33. If all or any part of the Shopping Center shall be appropriated or taken under the power of eminent domain by any public or quasi-public authority, Licensor shall be entitled to the entire award or compensation granted as a result thereof.

34. The failure of Licensor to insist upon strict performance by Licensee of any of the conditions, provisions, rules and regulations, and agreements in this License, or to exercise any option, shall not be deemed a waiver of any of Licensor's rights or remedies and shall not be deemed a waiver.

35. If either party shall be delayed or hindered in or prevented from the performance of any act required hereunder by reason of strikes, lockouts, labor troubles, inability to procure materials, failure of power, restrictive governmental laws or regulations, riots, insurrection, war or other reason of a like nature not the fault of the party delayed in performing work or doing acts required under the terms of this License, then performance of any such act shall be excused for the period of delay and the period for the performance of any such act shall be extended for a period equivalent to the period of such delay, provided, however, nothing contained herein shall limit Licensor's right to revoke this License.

36. The provisions of this agreement providing for liquidated damages or a percentage or dollar addition to actual costs and

Licensor   _____

Licensee   _____

(Continued)

expenses have been stated because the parties acknowledge that it will be impossible or extraordinarily difficult to fix the precise amount of damages if there is a failure of performance or breach of an obligation addressed in said paragraph. Accordingly, the parties have agreed to the liquidated damage or percentage or dollar addition set forth herein as a fair and reasonable means for establishing the damages and expenses that will be incurred if there is a failure of performance or a breach of an obligation. Without limiting the provisions subject to this agreement, the provisions of paragraphs 4, 5 and 31 shall be specifically included within the provisions of this paragraph.

Licensor:

By: (Signature)_____

(Print Name)_____

Its:_____

Licensee:

By: (Signature)_____

(Print Name)_____

Its:_____

If Licensee is a CORPORATION, an authorized officer must sign on behalf of the corporation and indicate the capacity in which he/she is signing. The License must be executed by the president or vice-president unless the bylaws or a resolution of the board of directors shall otherwise provide, in which event the bylaws or a certified copy of the resolution, as the case may be, must be attached to this License. Also, the appropriate corporate seal must be affixed.

Licensor _____

Licensee _____

Figure 4

```
┌─────────────────────────────────────────────────┐
│              WEEKLY SALES SHEETS                  │
│                                                   │
│      Please deliver sales sheet to the            │
│      administration                               │
│      office the first Monday of every week.       │
│                                                   │
│  Tenant Name:      _____  │
│  Week Reporting:   _____  │
│                                                   │
│  Monday:        $ _____   │
│  Tuesday:       $ _____   │
│  Wednesday:     $ _____   │
│  Thursday:      $ _____   │
│  Friday:        $ _____   │
│  Saturday:      $ _____   │
│  Sunday:        $ _____   │
│  TOTAL:         $ _____   │
│                                                   │
│         (Sales reported should not include Tax)   │
│                                                   │
│  I hereby certify that the above sales figures    │
│           are true and correct.                   │
│                                                   │
│  Tenant Signature:  _____   │
│  Date:              _____   │
└─────────────────────────────────────────────────┘
```

Sales Reports. The second key operational control is the sales report, which is turned in by specialty retailers on a monthly basis, perhaps on the tenth of the month. Often these are put onto a spreadsheet by the owner's staff, which can make sure that each specialty tenant remains roughly in a proper rent-to-sales ratio.

Bad Debt and Collections. Operating controls include a process for bad debt and collections. There should not be a lot of bad debt with specialty retailers. If a tenant cannot succeed at a center, then the cart or kiosk should simply be removed, with no debt collection needed. Often this will necessitate a buyout of the remaining term of the li-

Figure 5

MONTHLY SALES SHEETS

Please deliver monthly sales sheet to the administration office the first day of every calendar month.

Tenant Name: _____

Month Reporting: _____

Actual Sales: $ _____

(Sales reported should not include Tax)

I hereby certify that the above sales figures are true and correct.

Tenant Signature: _____

Date: _____

---

cense. In some cases, however, a tenant has been known to simply abandon the cart, in which case the owner must rely on a collection agency to collect past due.

Rules and Regulations. The specialty retailer should certainly get the same handbook of rules and regulations as the in-line tenants. The handbook will include all items not specified in the license: hours of operation, trash disposal, securing the cart, dress code, etc. Violation of these rules is often subject to fines.

Many malls are increasingly beset with hawking. Hawking occurs most often with retailers who are selling demonstrative products. The

Figure 6

SALES REPORT

Date: _____

Tenant Name: _____

Business Address: _____

City/State/Zip: _____

Business Phone: _____

Month/Year: _____

Gross Sales: $ _____

Signed: _____

Title: _____

Please deliver to Mall Office by the fifth of each month with any Percentage Rent
due.

employees often call out to or "hawk" customers, which is a violation
of the mall rules and is also subject to fines.

Visual Presentation. The cart or kiosk's visual presentation also is a
key control over the operation, and often a tricky one. The cart's visual staging can be done by in-house personnel or by an outside contractor—the mall budget will affect this. The license should specify a
start date for discussions on visual presentation, which should include
the specialty leasing rep, the tenant and the visual merchandiser,
whether in-house or contracted.

Figure 7

VISUAL MERCHANDISING PLAN

GENERAL PLAN
How much have you budgeted for visual display?
What is the value of your kiosk or MRU?
What is your MRU or kiosk profile?
THEME
What is the main theme of your kiosk or MRU during this season?
What is the focal point of your MRU or kiosk?
What are the dominant and the accent colors at your MRU and kiosk?
Do you require extra electricity? How much?
DESIGN
Do you use both vertical and horizontal display?
Do you use formal and compositional balance?
Do you start with dark colors and continue to the right or to the front with light colors?
Do you display the big items at the bottom and the small items at the top?
DISPLAY
Do you rotate the merchandise every week?
Do you increase the number of the facings for one product?
Do you display the specialty brands at the top level, the strong sales at the hip to eye level and the fast movers at the bottom level?
Are your shelves fully stocked?
SIGNS
Are your signs consistent in style and size?
Are your signs clean and visible?

(continued)

The goal of these discussions is to sketch out what the cart or kiosk is going to look like. Determine if the tenant has its own fixtures and whether these are acceptable within the mall's overall design plan. Often tenants have no clue how to merchandise the carts—all they

FIXTURES
Ground cover (texture, color, etc.)
T-stands
Fourways
Cube units
Risers (size, color, number)
Wire grids
Shelving
Crates
Cylinders
Showcases
PROPS
Textiles
Foamcore
Plywood
Glass
Wrapping paper, art papers
Mannequins
Natural materials, flowers
Antiques
Ribbons, braids and bows
Baskets, barrels and boxes
Decorative screens and panels

know is the product. The mall staff frequently will work with the cart retailer through every step of design, cart assembly and opening. Daily visits should be made to the cart to ascertain compliance with the license and the tenant handbook.

The Deal

PROSPECTING

The initial work of the specialty leasing rep, however, is in prospecting for tenants—that is where the deal begins. A good way to canvass for new tenants is to see what other malls are doing. Many companies suggest the specialty leasing reps do this at least one day a week. Leasing reps can leave business cards and leasing packets and try to get the other malls' tenants interested in opening another cart at their mall.

The mall office itself may get several walk-ins per week. It is helpful to supply the mall office with a list of the most desirable types of cart tenants. If a walk-in is in a desirable merchandise category, the office receptionist can contact the leasing rep right away. If the walk-in's merchandise is not on the list, the receptionist can offer an application and leasing packet, then the leasing rep can follow up later.

Leasing reps often have developed relationships with other reps at competitive malls in their market or with counterparts from within their company and will often share or refer tenants to one another.

A final prospecting tool is the telephone book. Match up the desirable categories with the listings in the telephone book and see if any of the outfits have considered a mall location or expanding to another.

DEAL TERMS

The deal also rests on its terms—the specifics that are written into the license. There is always a base rent. Normally, there is one fee for January through October, and then the fee increases for the holiday season on November 1. The cart tenant may balk at the November 1 bump-up date, since the sales volume does not really kick in until the Friday after Thanksgiving—"black Friday"—but the added sales in that last weekend or two of November are more than enough to justify the additional rent.

These rent schedules can vary for other reasons as well. A tenant at an outdoor lifestyle mall in a cooler climate, for example, might pay less during the winter months, somewhat more during the summer, and then have the holiday bump-up.

The deal terms will include overage rent or breakpoint rent. This is similar to the structure of in-line tenants, but the numbers may change. A breakpoint of 15 percent is not uncommon for carts and kiosks. If a cart has a breakpoint of $10,000 per month and only does $9,500 in March sales, then the tenant will pay no overage rent that month. If, however, the tenant does $12,000 in April sales, the tenant will pay 15 percent of the extra $2,000 (over the breakpoint), meaning the owner gets an additional $300 in overage rent.

Other charges may be built into the deal. Some owners charge a monthly visual merchandising fee—this is usually set simply to reimburse the cost of the visual merchandising contractor or staff. A one-time fee can be charged if a mall places a standard sign on the top of the cart. Some owners also charge an administrative fee or an application fee.

INCUBATING TENANTS

Some specialty tenants are brand-new to retailing. They may be entrepreneurs or just shoppers with a good idea. In those cases, the leasing rep may offer to "incubate" the tenant—literally work together with them to develop their concept and open their store.

In many cases, these incubated tenants and their great ideas will succeed to the extent that they seek additional locations, in the same mall or others. When a leasing rep finds an entrepreneur with a real knack for merchandising, the rep can even call on that cart owner to test other formats or types of items—the owner may end up leasing several carts or kiosks in the same center, each with a different merchandise line.

While the leases for carts or kiosks typically have a maximum and renewable term of 1 year, some merchandise types like cell phones simply perform better from a cart or kiosk than from an in-line store. In those cases, the owner or the retailer may seek a multiple-year deal that would justify a standard lease, even though the space is located in the common area.

8 | Tenant Coordination and Construction

Karen M. Scott, SCMD

What Is Tenant Coordination, and Who Performs It?

Tenant coordinators are the professionals who bridge the gap between the leasing team and property management. They work with the tenants to expedite store openings. The quicker tenant coordination and construction is done, the faster rent can commence, which results in increased value and profitability to a center.

The tenant coordinator's functions and duties vary depending upon the size of the developer and the types of properties in the firm's portfolio. Tenant coordination is not a recognized academic discipline, but experienced tenant coordinators are becoming increasingly sought after as lease deals get more complicated, particularly in power centers and mixed-use centers.

Development Team Requirements

Large developers typically have a dedicated team of professionals in a tenant coordination department, whereas small to medium developers might only have one person or might spread out tenant coordination functions among other team members.

LARGE DEVELOPERS WITH A DEDICATED TEAM
Large developers usually have a dedicated tenant coordination department. These staff members are professionally educated and experienced in architecture, construction or property management.

As the shopping center industry has matured, it has evolved from construction of all-new centers to extensive rehabilitation and renovation of existing centers. This has enhanced the role of the large developer's tenant coordination team because, as compared to tenant coordination in a new mall, it is more difficult to manage construction of a replacement tenant within the midst of an operating center or to handle the complexities of moving tenants while keeping others open during a center renovation.

Sometimes a large developer will separate tenant coordination functions by task or function. One person will work on developing construction criteria and plan review while another might be tasked administratively and a third oversees field construction.

SMALL TO MEDIUM DEVELOPERS WITH A DEDICATED PERSON

Small and medium-sized developers also provide tenant coordination to speed preopening activity, but they may only have one or two people on staff dedicated to it. As a result, the tenant coordinators must be multi-task-oriented, working on a wide variety of projects and products depending upon the developer's properties in the portfolio.

SMALL DEVELOPERS' TEAM MEMBERS SHARING JOB DUTIES

Sometimes small developers will parcel out the tenant coordination duties among existing staff members performing other critical functions. A paralegal, for example, might write an abstract of a lease for the construction personnel. A staff architect might do plan review of a tenant's plans and then hand them over to the facility manager, who will oversee construction. Property managers also often assume tenant coordination functions, including construction coordination and oversight and releasing allowances to tenants.

CONSULTANTS

Owners and developers will occasionally bring in outside consultants to assist in the tenant coordination process, especially if they have a lot of projects getting ready to open immediately and need professional assistance without wanting to staff up for the long run. Some municipalities have difficult permitting and entitlement processes, so developers may hire specialists to deal with those issues in order to assist the team and tenants through challenging bureaucratic processes.

Figure 1

Typical Tenant Coordination Departments		
Typical In-House Department, Large Developer for Malls and Lifestyle Centers (large volume of tenants, often multiple properties)	*Typical In-House Department, Small Developer for Power Centers, Neighborhood Centers and Lifestyle Centers (smaller volume of tenants, fewer properties)*	*Tenant Coordination, Outsource or Third Party for All Product Types (depending upon the needs of the department or developer)*
1. Architectural and sign review and approvals 2. Track status of plans, permits and construction 3. Answer questions for tenant design and construction teams and troubleshoot 4. Hand off to mall operations or field TC for construction oversight 5. Work as field representative during final days toward opening 6. Negotiate lease scope 7. Perform Construction Project Manager functions for landlord's work	1. Obtain tenant prototypical plans and specs and translate to landlord construction drawings for building and site as required 2. Lease negotiation, construction costs 3. Lease administration 4. Obtain approvals on plans with tenants 5. Oversee permitting process 6. Hire general contractor 7. Oversee turnover of store and associated site with all work completed as per the lease exhibits to store operations 8. Will visit site and troubleshoot problems and site-verify completion of work for tenants and landlord's contractors 9. Turn over tenant upon opening to property management team	1. Write design criteria 2. Review construction drawings 3. Fulfill administrative functions as designated by owner they are working for 4. Work as field associate overseeing compliance to landlord rules and regulations and adherence to approved plans 5. Field troubleshooting between tenant's and landlord's construction teams

The Relationship Between Tenant Coordination and Other Disciplines

THE CHANGING ROLE OF TENANT COORDINATORS

No one goes to school to learn how to become a tenant coordinator. Nor do most tenant coordinators start their shopping center careers in that field. Most come from other professional disciplines, including architecture, engineering, construction and facilities management. Sometimes a person decides to move into tenant coordination as a result of successful completion of a short-term field assignment. Others do so with a desire to explore new aspects of the retail industry. Contractors and architects often find their way into tenant coordination, appreciating the respect and fulfillment they receive from working as an owner's representative.

As a discipline, tenant coordination is changing from one that was primarily a construction function overseeing tenant construction into one that is a leasing function requiring knowledge of construction. The field is evolving in this way because successful store openings are depending less on construction skills and more on participating in the entire tenant coordination process. This process places emphasis on the ability to read and interpret leases, communicate effectively with tenants and protect the landlord by making sure lease obligations are met in a timely manner.

Tying the tenant coordination function more closely to leasing than construction seems to be working better for the tenants as well; they can go to one person to get problems resolved in construction, leasing and operations until store opening, when they are turned over to property management.

Communication skills are very important within the tenant coordination process. The tenant coordinator is constantly communicating and negotiating between the various groups involved in a store's opening. These groups can include the tenant's design and construction team, the landlord's design and construction team, facilities and property management and the municipality as well as other tenants who might be affected by nearby construction.

But while the field is morphing into more of a leasing function, its roots in construction cannot be overlooked. Tenant coordinators need to know the basics of design and construction, including how to read blueprints, communicate with tenant contractors and understand contractual obligations as well as the overall construction process.

Figure 2. Samples of organizational charts of how tenant coordinators can fit into a project or development team.

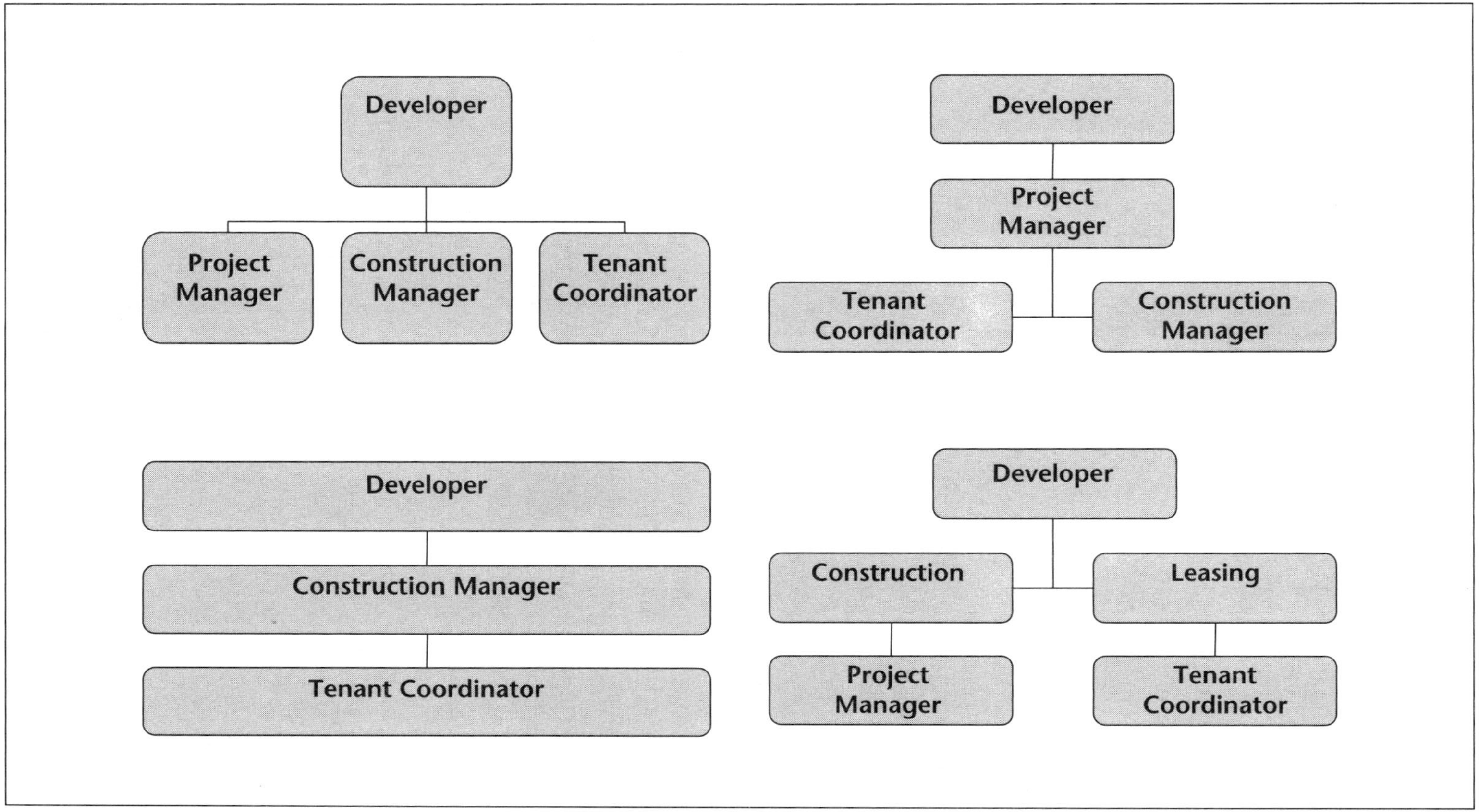

They also need to know to whom to turn for answers to critical questions. For instance, they might not need to know how many pounds of water pressure are needed in a particular automatic sprinkler system, but they do need to know who to call and ask about it.

ASSISTING THE LEASING TEAM: CONSTRUCTION COSTS AND DEAL RAMIFICATIONS

A landlord needs to understand how much it will cost to do a deal—this is an important aspect of a tenant coordinator's work. Tenant coordinators can assist the leasing team in putting together estimated construction costs—part of the landlord's obligations as part of doing a deal. Those costs get factored into the rent, tenant allowances and eventually the pro forma for a project.

Along with looking at the actual construction costs, experienced tenant coordinators are critical in asking key questions that the leasing team might not think of, but that can result in additional costs over and above expected construction costs.

As an example, a leasing agent might present to the team a deal to place a cigar shop in the middle of an existing and operating mixed-use building. The tenant coordinator would identify that the potential tenant might need an extensive back room and a very small lobby or vestibule as the prime sales area. Some of the questions the tenant coordinator would ask as part of identifying the potential challenges of placing the tenant in that location would be:

- "Doesn't a cigar shop have to dehumidify the stock?" That could mean upgrading the electrical service and finding a place to add more rooftop equipment.
- "Will there be a smoking room?" That means running additional ductwork through adjoining operating tenants to take the smoke to a special exhaust area away from a front door or another tenant's fresh air intake.

These questions would result in more expense and coordination than might ordinarily be expected.

The initial estimates help a leasing agent to determine if this potential deal is going to work within the pro forma currently projected for the center. Occasionally it will be determined that while the deal is costly, it is still a good one to do because of the new store's added value to the center's tenant mix and marketing goals. Strategic planning can deal with the deal complexities.

The initial estimates put forth by the tenant coordinator usually do not translate into formal budgets until after the development of actual construction plans, which usually occurs after the lease is signed. The initial estimates, however, assist the leasing agent and developer in making better-informed business decisions.

ASSISTING THE DEVELOPER: THE IMPACT OF THE DEAL

There are factors beyond finance and construction with which a tenant coordinator should be familiar—among them what impact a particular store would have on the shopping center as a whole and what, if any, impact there would be from community design guidelines as well as the overall center design and aesthetic.

Signage is a common area of concern. For example, the design concept for a sporting goods chain might have a goalpost that holds its sign up over the storefront. The tenant might require that the goalpost be 40 feet high to meet the corporate standard. The shopping center itself, however, might have an operating easement agreement that limits elevation heights to 36 feet. This issue would need to be flagged back to the developer, who might have to get special permission from other parties signatory to the operating easement agreement to allow this tenant the 40-foot height.

It is critical that a tenant coordinator look for and flag these kinds of issues so that they can be worked out prior to a lease being executed. Occasionally the tenant coordinator not only needs to identify the issue, but also help work to resolve it. Tenant coordinators do not want to be known as "deal killers" by their leasing associates; instead they want to assist the agents in creating value for a property while protecting the leasing team's valuable relationships with tenants in order to do future deals.

ASSISTING THE CONSTRUCTION MANAGEMENT TEAM: THE TENANT'S NEEDS

Generally, most people in construction would rather be on a job site kicking dirt and building things than dealing with the tenants directly. Construction people are not attracted to the details of the leasing deal—they are not deal makers. Their involvement with the lease extends as

Figure 3

TENANT ABSTRACT
SMITH'S TOWN STORE

Tenant Name:	Smith's Town Store, LLC
Address:	Smith's Town Store 2300 Regency Place Park, Suite 3500 Atlanta, GA 30326 Attention: Real Estate
Others for Notices:	Joseph Brown, Esq. Brown, Group and Jones, LLP 1500 Peachtree Center Avenue, N.E. Atlanta, GA 30303 And James Adler Construction Manager 2300 Regency Place Park, Suite 3500 Atlanta, GA 30326
Size:	3,000 sf, size certification not required unless requested by tenant within 5 days of delivery.
Location:	J520
Date of Execution:	3/20/05
Lease Commencement:	The first to occur of 90 days from the day of delivery or date tenant opens.
Delivery Information:	Pre-delivery notice due 30 days prior, delivery notice day of delivery.
Plan Submission:	Within 30 days from lease execution. Landlord has 10 days to respond and comment. Tenant has 15 days to address.
Landlord's Responsibility:	White box, see construction exhibit.
Utilities:	Upon delivery.
Signage:	No pylon, mall directory allowed, coming soon banners allowed.
Exclusivity:	None.
Tenant Inducement or Allowance	$120,000 evidence of work satisfactorily completed, reasonable evidence all work is paid for, all liens satisfied or waived, open one month, tenant not in default, estoppel, tenant in good standing
Chargebacks:	Landlord has right to charge back for signage directory, awnings and additional work as per requested by tenant with 15% administration fee.
Approvals:	Tenant can install satellite, landlord to approve location.
Blackout:	Tenant not required to open between August 15 and September 15, November 1 and January 15.
Closeout:	Landlord and tenant must walk space 10 days after letter sent out; LL has 15 days to complete outstanding items—tenant must give LL list within 30 days.

far as understanding its impact on construction. Therefore, they appreciate a savvy tenant coordinator who understands construction needs as well as the tenant's requirements.

This is important both in new construction and in the renovation of an entire mall. Tenant coordinators in those situations might have a dozen or more tenants with whom they are dealing, each of them with their own separate requirements and demands. The tenant coordinator's role is to master an understanding of those needs and communicate them to the construction team.

ASSISTING THE TENANT: BUILDING REQUIREMENTS AND MUNICIPAL RULES

Tenant coordinators must understand the building's infrastructure and give the tenants important information for design and construction in order to seamlessly place that new store into the midst of the shopping center infrastructure. Especially critical is mechanical, electrical and plumbing information, since these systems can impact not only the new tenant, but other tenants around them. A tenant that does not properly understand the chilled water system for a building can end up creating enormous damage to the entire infrastructure. It is up to the tenant coordinator not only to convey the information, but to put systems into place to oversee construction on these critical systems and to test and make sure connections are done correctly.

Tenant coordinators also bring immense value to tenants by alerting them to design criteria required by the center, freight elevator and loading dock use and requirements and special construction requirements. For instance, in parts of the country prone to hurricanes, there will be wind load requirements on rooftop equipment and exterior storefront systems. The tenant coordinator assists both the landlord and the tenants by passing this information back to the tenants and by making sure the tenants' plans comply with both the owner's documents and the municipality's requirements.

The relationships and experience that tenant coordinators have with the municipality can also be of great interest and value to a tenant. Since tenant coordinators work with a variety of stores, over time they can identify, through plan review and construction, "hot issues" with the building department. By passing this information back to tenants, they can save the tenants' time in permitting and construction.

If experienced tenant coordinators are working on the predevelopment of a new center or renovation of an older one, they can often identify potential issues in advance that will aid the successful opening of new stores. These issues can be built into the overall project schedule or negotiated in advance with the municipality.

Figure 4

Typical MEP Requirements			
Types of Systems	*High-End Specialty Center*	*Regional Mall*	*Community Center*
Mechanical	Closed circulating systems, high-pressure high-rise, limited tie-ins and extensive testing, limited availability to fresh air and exhaust	Closed circulating systems that require inspected taps by field team, limited tie-ins to fresh air or exhaust, or stand-alone rooftop systems feed spaces	Individually mounted rooftop systems
Electrical	Specific guidelines to overall watts; limited availability of power, will need connection into landlord distribution center	Specific guidelines to overall watts; limited availability of power, might need connection by designated sub into distribution box	Generally comes from landlord meter room or separate riser; might be limited availability of power due to riser size or transformer size
Plumbing	Shutoff valve in ceiling with limited use, no availability to upgrade the size of line for additional water flow	Shutoff valve in ceiling with limited use, limited availability to upgrade the size of line, might be submetered	Typically independently metered, can upgrade size of water line and meter if use changes, subject to impact fees
Fire Alarm	Information on type of fire alarm system, location and compatibility of devices and if there is a designated contractor	Information on type of fire alarm system, location and compatibility of devices and if there is a designated contractor	Information on type of fire alarm system, location and compatibility of devices and if there is a designated contractor
Automatic Sprinkler Protection	Information on tie-in locations, existing plans and designated contractor	Information on tie-in locations, existing plans and designated contractor and shutdown requirements	Information on tie-in locations, existing plans and designated contractor or shutdown requirements

(continued)

Typical MEP Requirements			
Types of Systems	High-End Specialty Center	Regional Mall	Community Center
Telecom	High-rises might have own telecom room and service provider	Might be designated provider, or tenant provides wiring and equipment and runs back to central distribution points in landlord rooms	Pedestal from local provider to landlord distribution area or to tenant space; tenant provides equipment and wiring back to distribution area or direct to pedestal
Type of information conveyed to tenant and their design team	Recommend landlord engineering team convey information to tenant architects and engineers and review information from tenants to ensure tenant utilizes only what is available and provides direction to general contractor for testing and tie-in compliance	If extensive coordination with landlord systems required, generally in multi-level center, then engineering team conveys information and review. If single-story mall with mostly stand-alone systems, the MEP plans and roof framing plans can be conveyed. Shop drawings for sprinkler system might be available.	Shell plans with MEP info showing any tie-in locations, a roof framing plan and MEP plans showing any existing equipment or landlord-provided equipment. If it is an existing center, then tenant field verification must be required.

ASSISTING PROPERTY MANAGEMENT AND OPERATIONS: SHORTENING THE LEARNING CURVE

By the close of any project, the tenant coordinators probably know more about the project than anyone. Such information includes the tenants and their requirements, life safety systems, sprinkler shutdowns, roof types and more. This information is invaluable to the members of the property management team, since it will shorten their learning curve as they take over management of the center and assume the relationship with the now-open tenant.

The Tenant Coordination Process

Effective tenant coordination starts before the lease is signed.

CONSTRUCTION EXHIBITS

Leasing agents who rely on their tenant coordination associates to review and comment on construction exhibits before deals are done are protecting the interests of their developers and owners efficiently. Tenant coordinators who understand the construction process can identify items that can cost the landlord money. Such simple things as the size of a water line or the condition of a concrete slab can end up costing a landlord or developer hundreds of thousands of dollars in remediation work.

In addition to reading and commenting on exhibits, tenant coordinators are occasionally called upon to write construction exhibits and design criteria for new projects. This information, compiled early, can assist not only the leasing team in identifying reasonable rent figures, but also the design team in creating construction documents that reflect what the landlord has determined they can afford to do based on leases already signed or being negotiated.

TENANT CONSTRUCTION REQUIREMENTS AND OBLIGATIONS

Once exhibits are agreed upon and criteria are written, the tenant coordinator then begins the process of creating documents that meet the requirements of the lease. If the landlord is providing a "black box," "white box" or "build to suit," the tenant coordinator needs to convey that to the design team and have them create working documents from which the tenants design and the landlord builds.

This can trigger a lengthy approval process with tenants. If the landlord is responsible for extensive construction obligations such as a build-to-suit for a big box tenant, then there might be several plan checks and resubmittals required until the tenant signs off on the construction plans. The landlord themselves might require extensive plan reviews and resubmittals with tenants to whom they are giving black box work, ensuring that the tenant design team understands the building infrastructure requirements and design strategy. This will give the landlord the look they expect in terms of quality and tenant presentation.

Along with reviewing construction plans, tenant coordinators also review signage to make sure it conforms to the criteria for the center and/or the municipality.

If tenants do not provide plans or information in a timely manner, tenant coordinators are often the first to flag potential default issues. Leasing and management teams that take heed of the tenant coordinator's warnings can often save themselves a lot of legal costs by getting rid of a problem tenant early.

Along with plan review, tenant coordinators also assist the tenant teams by answering construction questions and by encouraging tenants to get into permitting as soon as possible. Tenant coordinators with strong relationships with the municipality can add value not only to the tenant and landlord, but also to the municipality by effectively communicating information that can expedite the permitting time.

Once tenants are ready to start construction, tenant coordinators who watch the process and effectively troubleshoot construction issues can assist in stores getting open in a more efficient and timely manner, thus adding immense value to a project by creating income early. They also assist the contractors, who are making money since they have finished the work quickly, as well as the tenant, who is now open for business and selling.

Figure 5

Typical Signage Requirements			
Types of Signage	*High-End Specialty Center*	*Regional Mall*	*Community Center*
Exterior signage	Halo-lit, concealed neon, sandblasted glass, metallic leaf, routed signs with push-through letters	Halo-lit, concealed neon, sandblasted glass, routed signs with push-through letters, individually mounted, channel letters, tied into landlord's time clock, no raceways	No box signs, individually mounted channel letters, raceways acceptable if painted to match facade, professionally produced and installed
Interior signage	Dimensionally designed and artistic signs; translucent posters on lightboxes	Professionally made, no handwritten signs, no running LED reader boards visible through storefront	Professionally made, no handwritten signs

The Primary Function of a Tenant Coordinator

INITIATE THE INCOME FLOW

The primary function of a tenant coordinator is to get income coming in. Specifically, it is to make sure all parties meet all obligations related to the commencement of rent in a timely manner.

Landlord obligations are determined by the construction obligations stated in the lease. If a tenant coordinator can assist a tenant in expediting a store opening, then sometimes rent can be triggered earlier than the amount of buildout time stated in the lease. For instance, if the lease calls for rent to commence after a 90-day construction period or the day the store opens for business (whichever occurs earlier), and the tenant is able to open in 75 days, then rent will commence 15 days earlier.

This not only adds additional money to the rental stream but also to the total value of the property in the owner's portfolio. Early store openings also add value to a center due to the fresh nature of the tenants' presentation and any marketing and promotional value they bring with them.

PROTECTING THE LANDLORD FROM LEASE PENALTIES

To protect themselves from tying up space and losing income, landlords will insert penalties in leases for underperforming tenants. Tenant coordinators need to keep a close watch on tenants' progress and make sure they are doing what it takes to open in a timely manner. Problem tenants can be weeded out and flagged early in the process by a vigilant tenant coordinator.

Tenants also put penalties into the lease to protect themselves from landlords' nonperformance. Generally, the bigger the tenant, the larger those penalties might be. Sometimes termination clauses can also kick in. These penalties can range from a one-time fee to a day-by-day free-rent charge or lump-sum liquidated damages. Most of these penalties are designed to recover damages from the landlord for tying up resources that cost the tenant money, such as ordering seasonal merchandise, advertising and payroll.

There also are other implications to late delivery that could affect the landlord, such as co-tenancy clauses that prohibit rent from other tenants kicking in. Tenant coordinators who watch for these types of hidden clauses usually not found in the construction exhibits do much to make sure that a development team has enough information to make important scheduling decisions and financial decisions.

MAINTAINING STANDARDS AND PROTECTING SYSTEMS

Retail contractors occasionally damage a landlord's facilities and finishes. Retail contractors are hired to come in and do a job quickly, and as such do not always take care of the landlord's properties. Retailers are not always aware when one of their subcontractors damages the landlord's property. Some of this damage could be minor, such as damaged asphalt or bushes that are uprooted and not replanted. Some of it can be substantial, though, and can affect a key mechanical system, void a critical roof warranty or cause a landlord to be heavily fined by local or federal authorities. It is up to the tenant coordinator to create rules and regulations to protect the landlord and other tenants and to enforce them.

Tenant coordinators also do this by making sure that design criteria requirements are met during the plan preview process and in construction. A mall storefront that does not match up into a bulkhead correctly can be an eyesore, whereas a flooring transition from the mall to the tenant's space not smoothly handled can become a trip hazard.

Not only does this protect the landlord's facilities, the public and other tenants, but it also helps to maintain a high standard for the center itself, which increases its appeal to customers and prospective tenants. Once a store opens for business, it becomes property management's job to make sure that store maintains a fresh and exciting appearance. Tenant coordinators, however, can also assist in keeping a center looking fresh by letting management know which retailers are looking tired. Perhaps fixtures need to be updated or replaced, or unsightly storage removed from open window areas. There may be dirt and dust in windows, handwritten signs or exterior signage not functioning correctly.

Other Functions of a Tenant Coordinator

While the role of a tenant coordinator is to protect landlord interests by overseeing tenant construction and plan review and to expedite store openings, savvy landlords realize that tenant coordinators also can add value in other ways.

LEASING AND DEVELOPER FUNCTIONS

Tenant coordinators are responsible for understanding the implications and possible impact of a lease. Tenant coordinators are brought in early by the leasing team to help assess the impact of potential deals. In doing so, they add immense value to a developer's team by providing cost estimates, pinpointing issues that impact site design and construction, creating permitting plans with local municipalities, adding input to project schedules, and identifying and negotiating exterior building elevations as part of the approval process.

Experienced tenant coordinators also bring to the table plenty of "end-game" experience from other projects that helps the project team identify issues that could hinder successful and timely completion of a new project.

An experienced tenant coordinator also helps the leasing team by writing construction exhibits and design criteria early and giving them to the design team. With those, the leasing team has a much better idea of what the tenant will get, instead of waiting for the full construction drawings, done much later in the development process.

THE LANDLORD REPRESENTATIVE FUNCTION

Tenant coordinators earn respect from both the development team and from the tenant's design and construction teams if they make sure all parties are well informed, communicate obligations and expectations efficiently and can resolve conflict. Since the prime directive for most tenant coordinators is to get stores open for business, they are often willing to make difficult decisions quickly and are motivated to involve parties who can help make those decisions in order to keep both landlord and tenant construction moving.

They are often seen as the "go-to" person not only by the tenants and their teams, but also by the municipality, since they manage large amounts of construction being done by various parties with different agendas and goals but within the confines of one area.

Tenant coordinators are also the enforcers who make sure that the tenants comply with requirements that protect the physical facility or its design aesthetic. They review tenant plans and check for utility loads and design issues to make sure the tenant design team understands exactly what the landlord is providing or requires. They also need to protect the interest of the developer by making sure the project team fully understands all the obligations of a lease. They also protect the interests of operating tenants by making sure that any adjoining or nearby construction is not hampering or impairing them from doing business during normal operating hours.

A RESOURCE AND ADVISOR TO TENANTS

The landlord–tenant relationship is often confrontational. A tenant coordination team that sees its role as a tenant advisor and advocate, however, can do much more to help tenants create a dynamic sales atmosphere in a timely, cost-efficient manner.

Developers want particular tenants introduced into their store mix due to each tenant's retail strategy and success. Tenant coordinators who remember this and respect the tenant's brands while working with them through the design, permitting and construction process are much more efficient than tenant coordinators who are inflexible and want to fight. They also become invaluable assets to the leasing team. If all projects are equal, with none having superiority in location, rent or appeal, then tenants are going to be more likely to go with a landlord who looks out after their interests and respects their brand than landlords who do not.

Typically, tenant coordinators do the following:

1. Review tenant plans for conformance to landlord criteria and negotiate solutions to problems
2. Oversee tenant contractors to make sure work is timely and in compliance with landlord rules and regulations
3. Function as a liaison between the landlord's and tenant's design and construction teams
4. Work as a liaison between the municipality and the tenant design and construction team

TEAM MEMBER FOR LANDLORD CONSTRUCTION AND PROPERTY MANAGEMENT

Tenant coordinators bring value to the landlord's construction and property management teams. Tenant coordinators take on some of the annoying details that the construction and leasing team does not want to handle. They are administrators who read leases and deal with many details and obligations. They assimilate those details into meaningful schedules and dates. They identify potential impacts of leases and cost issues, which frees leasing to go out and do more deals armed with the best possible knowledge that their deals are profitable.

Tenant coordinators bring knowledge of what tenants want and expect in the lease, allowing the project management team to make good design decisions. They have effective negotiating skills that assist landlord and tenant design teams to honor both the landlord's vision for the center and the tenant's branding and logo requirements. They protect landlord systems and bird-dog tenant construction, freeing the landlord operations and property managers to concentrate on running their centers instead of policing construction. Most of all, tenant coordinators help maintain important relationships for the leasing team as well as create value by getting tenants open for business quicker.

9 | Negotiating
Steve Weingarten

Leasing, negotiating and deal-making in general are as much art as science. The human factor is as important as lease clauses in getting a good deal. Successful leasing reps have a palette of styles and approaches to use in lease negotiations and quickly learn to set aside some nonproductive behaviors.

Win/Win

It is a fallacy to think that negotiating always means that one person wins and the other person loses. The test of a truly successful negotiation is that both parties walk away with a win. Clearly, in almost every negotiation, someone has the advantage. The key to successful negotiation is how one uses or abuses that advantage, for later on, in that transaction or in the next one, or some years in the future, the once-disadvantaged party will remember his or her treatment by the advantaged party and the future deal may be doomed from the start. This would be complicated, of course, if the once-disadvantaged party had the upper hand in the second lease deal.

The first step to successful negotiation is research—first about the landlord's needs and then about the retailer. For each prospective tenant, the leasing representative should determine the importance of that store to the shopping center. Does the center need this retailer, or is more likely that the retailer needs the location? Will the tenant help attract other tenants? Does the tenant fill a specific niche in the center? Research prior to the first contact with a potential tenant is helpful in achieving a win/win. The prospective tenant's Web site should be studied, at the very least.

It is helpful as well, when one meets the prospective tenant, to ask questions of a probing nature, rather than questions that might be answered with a "yes" or "no." More will be learned with those open-ended questions. Instead of, "Would you like to lease in my shopping center?"—which could generate a yes/no response—the leasing rep could ask, "What would be the ideal retail location for you?" or "What do you look for in a location?" Other topics might be the demographics the retailer wants, the co-tenancy, the visibility, the income levels, etc.

Listen and Be Quiet

To get the most out of those probing questions, of course, the leasing rep needs to listen to the response. Listening means paying attention to more than the words. One should assess body language, hesitancy and the retailer's confidence. Sometimes, too, the most important things are left unsaid. The leasing rep needs to focus on the prospective tenant, not on what the next topic in the conversation should be.

After one asks a question, it pays to be quiet—that is part of the listening. One cannot effectively talk and listen at the same time. It is okay to be silent in a negotiation—it might mean that someone is thinking, which is not a sign of weakness.

By asking the open-ended probing question, and by listening and being quiet, one can begin to ferret out the other person's objections to proceeding with the negotiation. Often, the best response to the concern is to write it down rather than to try to deal with the objection immediately. The leasing rep should not be afraid of objections—it is better to hear the objections early on than later. When a prospective tenant voices an objection, the leasing rep should repeat it back in slightly different words, so the tenant knows the objection was heard. Sometimes repeating it back will encourage the tenant to expand on the substance of the concern, and that is good.

In some cases, the leasing rep can list some positive things that respond to the prospective tenant's concern. In others, he or she can offer some benefits in other areas that outweigh the actual objection—a location next to the most popular store, for example, might distract the tenant from a shortage of parking spaces immediately outside the space being looked at. The leasing rep in that situation might offer to talk to the other stores and ask them to have their employees park in the rear of the lot, so close-up parking spaces can be saved for customers. Handle objections politely, but do not dismiss them.

Good Cop, Bad Cop

Good cop, bad cop is a familiar term in negotiation language, but it is very often transparent. Its useful role in lease negotiation is when the boss's approval is required. The boss, essentially, plays the role of the bad guy. Perhaps the boss can be brought into a meeting where he or she expresses concern about some of the aspects of the proposed deal. When the boss leaves the room, the leasing rep may have gained an advantage in seeking a common ground with the prospective tenant. The leasing rep in these situations positions himself or herself as the tenant advocate to the boss. This technique can also be used in conference calls.

One can also use this as a stalling technique—the leasing rep can say, "I'd better go ask my boss"—if the rep thinks a delay will bring the prospective tenant to a more reasonable point of view.

Relationships

Gaining trust in negotiations rests on relationships. Those built on mutual respect and trust can last for years, even decades, laying the groundwork for many leasing deals in the future. A leasing rep seeking to build a relationship with a prospective tenant might refer the tenant to other retailers or vendors with whom the leasing rep has built lasting relationships, as evidence of the leasing rep's authenticity and fairness.

To build a strong relationship with a potential tenant, the leasing rep must act in part as a tenant advocate. One should not act more firmly than need be, nor more flexibly. Authenticity is the key, and it will help both parties get through the rough stretches in the negotiation. Friendships may not work to mutual advantage in a business relationship, but finding common interests outside business often proves helpful.

Explain Reasons for Your Position

No kid likes hearing, "No, because I said so." Tenants do not like the phrase any more than kids do. If the tenant rep must say no to something—a lease clause, perhaps—the retailer deserves a good reason and will certainly expect one. The prospective tenant can relay the reason to his or her own boss, saving face back at the office and sustaining a respectful relationship with the leasing rep. When possible, pair the no with some other benefit or concession that will make the no less painful.

This concept applies to internal dealings as well, and in situations when the leasing rep is on the receiving end of the no. When the corporate attorneys return a marked-up lease, the leasing rep can sit down with them and have them explain why changes were made. In the best-case scenario, the leasing rep will explain why a clause is needed and can get it for the retailer. In the worst-case scenario, the attorneys' explanation will be the leasing rep's reason for giving the no.

Real Estate Committee

The authority of the real estate committee (or comparable deal-approving body) can work in the good cop, bad cop mode for the leasing rep. The rep can say to the tenant, "My real estate committee will never approve of that" or "I need to check with my real estate committee to get such-and-so." The real estate committee can also be used as a delaying tactic to soften the tenant's position on a given item. Again, this approach should be used only when it is authentic. Telling the truth all the time means that leasing reps never have to recall what their position was in the past.

Time and deadlines are important factors as well, particularly for the leasing rep. Many companies have regularly scheduled meetings of the real estate committees and leasing reps want to get proposed deals to them for review in time. Some companies grant bonuses at the end of a quarter and are amazed by how many deals get finalized in the final week of the quarter.

To be sure, the urgency factor should not be left until deadline time or the end of the quarter. Wasted time kills deals. The tenant should feel a sense of urgency throughout the negotiation—which is usually welcomed by the tenant, since an earlier store opening means quicker sales volume.

Glossary

abatement period [LEASING] A period of time during which the landlord defers or reduces rent or other payments, as an incentive to a tenant to open at the earliest possible time or for another purpose.

absorption (rate) [LEASING] The percentage of a particular type of real estate that can be sold or leased in a particular location during a certain period of time. The change in total space occupied or leased.

abstract [LEASING/LEGAL] A summary. A shortened version outlining the main points of a document.

additional rent [LEASING/ACCOUNTING] An amount beyond minimum rent, including reimbursements to the landlord for repairs and attorneys' fees.

agent [LEASING/INSURANCE/RISK MANAGEMENT] 1. A person or company licensed to represent one or several insurance companies. 2. A person or company involved in leasing, selling, or managing real estate, often known as leasing agents, real estate brokers and managing agents.

allowance [LEASING/LEGAL] Landlord contribution to tenant improvements. *See* also tenant allowance.

annual basic rental [ACCOUNTING/LEASING] The annual rent per square foot, one-twelfth due on the first day of each month.

annual percentage rent [ACCOUNTING/LEASING] A percentage of tenant's sales over a predetermined sales threshold.

appraisal rent [ACCOUNTING/LEASING] An amount based on sales potential as affected by the appraisal of a property at a given point in time; sometimes used interchangeably with *market rent*.

assignee [LEASING/LEGAL] New tenant that assumes the rights and responsibilities of the original tenant under the existing lease. Landlord approval is usually required.

assignment [LEASING/LEGAL] The transfer to another party of all a tenant's interests in a lease for the remainder of the lease term. It is distinguished from a sublease, in which some portion of the terms of the lease remains with the primary tenant.

back of the house or **back room** [OPERATIONS/LEASING] Nonselling area of a store that includes stockrooms, rest rooms, etc.

base rent [ACCOUNTING/LEASING] *See* minimum rent.

big box [LEASING/RETAIL] A single-use store, typically between 10,000 to 100,000 square feet or more, such as a large bookstore, office-supply store, pet store, electronics store or toy store.

blackout period [LEASING] A period of time when a tenant is able to delay an opening because it is too close to a holiday period and therefore too costly for that tenant to open; also called a dark period.

breakpoint [ACCOUNTING/MARKETING] Sometimes referred to as natural or actual breakpoint. In percentage rent, the point at which rent due from a specific percentage of sales equals the minimum rent.

   Theoretically, the point at which a tenant breaks even on expenses and sales, and thereafter begins to make a profit (a percentage of which is sometimes required to be paid to the landlord); also called a *sales breakpoint* or *natural breakpoint. See* unnatural breakpoint.

broker [LEASING] A licensed insurance professional who represents and acts on behalf of clients rather than an insurance company.

brokerage [LEASING/FINANCE] 1. The business of being a broker. 2. The commission received by a broker for his services.

budgeted rent [ACCOUNTING/LEASING] An amount based on sales potential, and representing the target approved by ownership for its annual plan; sometimes used interchangeably with **market rent.**

bump back store [LEASING] A white box, or temporary store space, built about four to eight feet back from the front of a vacant store space.

buyout [LEASING] Funds provided to enable operating management to acquire a tenant that is underperforming to replace it with a more productive tenant.

cancellation clause or "kickout clause" [LEASING/LEGAL] A contract provision that gives the right to terminate obligations upon the occurrence of specified conditions or events.

cap [ACCOUNTING/LEASING] A maximum amount that a tenant must pay for certain expenses, no matter how much they actually increase; usually a set amount or a percentage of increase.

captive brand stores [LEASING/RETAIL] Outlets selling brands that are not traded anywhere except in their own stores.

cart [LEASING/RETAIL] A merchandising display unit for a temporary tenant. Carts, often known as pushcarts or retail merchandising units (RMUs), are mobile, usually metal and/or wooden, and sometimes supplemented with fixtures to provide the tenant with adequate display areas.

cash-wrap [LEASING/RETAIL] The front counter/check-out area of a store or retail merchandising unit (RMU) that houses the cash register and wrapping section.

circulation plan [LEASING/OPERATIONS] A diagram showing the expected route customers take throughout a store or project. In a store, it determines the location of fixtures, displays and counters to ensure maximum exposure of merchandise to a maximum number of customers.

cold dark shell [LEASING] Term for unfinished space leased to a tenant, for which the tenant is responsible for paying all costs of construction.

commencement date [LEASING/LEGAL] The day on which a tenant's lease term begins; not to be confused with occupancy date.

common area units [LEASING] Several types of stand-alone displays occupying the common area of a center. *See* **also** kiosk; retail merchandising unit (RMU).

comparative lease analysis   [FINANCE/LEASING] A method of quantifying the economic differences between a proposed lease and a baseline, such as the development pro forma, for the same space.

competing business   [LEASING/GENERAL] A policy that limits tenant from opening competitive stores in the vicinity (within 50 miles) of the shopping center. Protects landlord from a reduced percentage rent; commonly referred to as *radius restriction*.

concession   [LEASING] The privilege of maintaining a subsidiary business within certain premises.

construction allowance   [FINANCE/LEASING] Money or financial incentives given to tenants for the cost of constructing their store space in a center.

Consumer Price Index (CPI)   [ACCOUNTING/LEASING] An indicator of rising prices or inflation used to measure the impact of inflation upon consumers; published by the Bureau of Labor Statistics at the end of every month.

Various statistical indexes gathered and published by the federal government as economic indicators.

The most widely known of many such measures of price levels and inflation that are reported to the U.S. government. It measures and compares, from month to month, the total cost of a statistically determined "typical market basket" of goods and services consumed by U.S. households.

Consumer Price Index adjustment (CPI)   [ACCOUNTING/LEASING] An adjustment to agreed-upon tenant charges such as marketing contributions based on changes in a consumer price index, generally released by government entities.

Consumer Price Index rents   [LEASING] Rents that are pegged to rises in the Consumer Price Index.

co-tenancy   [LEASING] A term that refers to a clause inserted into a tenant's lease stipulating that a reduced rent or no rent be paid until an agreed-upon percentage of the center is occupied.

coterminous   [LEASING] Lease terms that are the same.

credit tenants   [LEASING] Generally, national chains with strong financial balance sheets, to which an appraiser might apply a different rate, based on lower risk, than to smaller, undercapitalized local operators.

cumulative attraction   [MARKETING/LEASING] Refers to the sales advantage generated when two or more compatible retailers group together.

custom units   [LEASING] Various types of common area units, usually provided by the specialty retailer.

demising   [LEASING] Generally used to determine the separation of tenant spaces. Walls that separate tenant space.

double net lease   [LEASING/LEGAL] A lease in which the lessee pays rent to the lessor, as well as all taxes and insurance expenses that arise from the use of the property. The lessor pays maintainance expenses.

draw tenant   [MARKETING/LEASING] A store that attracts a large volume of customers to the center.

effective date   [LEASING/LEGAL] The latest date appearing on the signature page of the lease and the date upon which the lease contract goes into effect. *See* commencement date.

effective rent   [LEASING/GENERAL] A combination of the minimum and percentage rent paid by a tenant.

end cap   [LEASING/GENERAL] The ends of a strip center, whether the configuration is linear, L-shaped, U-shaped or other.

exclusive rights   [LEASING/LEGAL] Guarantee that a specific category of merchandise will be sold only by a certain store.

exclusives   [LEASING/LEGAL] A term referring to a store's being given the exclusive right to sell a particular category of merchandise within a shopping center.

An existing tenant may have negotiated the right to be the only one in the center to offer particular goods or services, and therefore space may not be leased to another tenant offering the same goods or services in competition with the first tenant.

exclusivity clause   [LEASING] A lease clause that limits the number of stores that can open in the shopping center competing with the lessee.

executed lease   [LEASING/LEGAL] A lease that has been signed by all parties and delivered.

exhibits   [LEASING/LEGAL] Attachments, usually to the end of an original lease, specifying the location, legal description, and tenant's construction specifications.

expiration date   [LEASING/LEGAL] The date on which a tenant's lease term is complete.

fixed CAM   [LEASING/ACCOUNTING] An agreed-upon rate negotiated between a landlord and tenant representing the tenant's share of common area maintainance. The initial rate may be increased annually by a percentage, generally in the 3 to 5 percent range. While fixed CAM covers all operating expenses other than taxes and all-risk insurance, certain expenses are occasionally excepted, such as liability insurance, utilities and snow removal.

fixed minimum rent   [ACCOUNTING/LEASING] Also known as *base rent.* The amount of basic rent paid by the tenant, usually stated as an amount per square foot charged on an annual basis. This figure does not include any other fees or assessments typically charged in a shopping center.

flat CAM   [LEASING/ACCOUNTING] A fixed tenant-occupancy charge in addition to base minimum rent, which may include nearly all additional costs, such as marketing and CAM. Excluded may be insurance, utilities and real estate taxes, which are not usually under the landlord's control. Flat CAM may be escalated on an annual agreed-upon rate such as the Consumer Price Index (CPI). *See also* fixed CAM.

flat rent   [ACCOUNTING/LEASING] A specific rent on square footage paid by a tenant for a specified period of time.

free rent   [LEASING] A period of occupancy by a tenant when no rent is charged.

frontage   [LEASING/GENERAL] The amount of space, in linear feet, of a tenant store that is exposed to the common area of a shopping center, increasing the store's exposure and visibility.

graduated lease   [LEASING/ACCOUNTING] A lease that provides for graduated changes, at stated intervals, in the amount of rent.

gross floor area   [LEASING/GENERAL] The total floor space of all buildings in a project.

gross leasable area (GLA)   [GENERAL] Normally the total area on which a shopping center leases to tenants or is available for lease. The GLA includes all selling space as well as storage and other miscellaneous space.

The square footage of a shopping center that can generate income by being leased to tenants. This figure does not include the area occupied by department stores or anchor users if such anchors own their own site and the area is not leased from the shopping center.

The measurement used to define how much space a tenant has leased in a center. GLA is determined by measuring the distance between the middle walls of a space and the distance between front outside wall to back outside wall.

The total floor area designed for tenant occupancy and exclusive use, including basements, mezzanines and upper floors. It is measured from the center line of joint partitions and from outside wall faces.

gross lease [LEASING] A lease in which the landlord pays 100 percent of all taxes, insurance, and maintenance associated with the operation of a shopping center.

guarantor [LEASING] A third party in the landlord/tenant relationship whose credit standing is used to guarantee the tenant's performance or lease obligations.

guaranty [LEASING/GENERAL] Assurance of performance by one party of another party's obligation.

holdover [LEASING/LEGAL] When a tenant remains in possession of the premises after its term has ended; the landlord can evict the tenant or bind it to another term. A holdover provision in a lease usually requires the tenant's rent to escalate significantly at the expiration of the lease.

incubation [LEASING] The process of assisting a nonpermanent tenant in developing into a permanent one over a period of time.

incubator tenants [LEASING] Specialty leasing tenants (also known as temporary tenants) often need incubation before they are financially strong enough or experienced enough to have a long-term lease.

initial assessment [ACCOUNTING/LEASING] A one-time assessment, equal to one year's dues, charged to new tenants in addition to the standard merchants' association annual dues.

in-line store [LEASING/GENERAL] A retail outlet placed contiguous to neighboring retailers such that their frontages are in a straight line and behind what is considered the leaseline. Tenants operating in the common area are not considered in-line.

key money [FINANCE/LEASING] Money from the tenant to the landlord for the right to operate a business in the center.

kick-out clause [LEASING/LEGAL] An option that allows a landlord or tenant to terminate the lease before the end of the term. In the tenant's case, generally tied to the presence of another retailer. *See* cancellation clause.

kiosks [LEASING/GENERAL] Booths located in the common areas of the center or mall and generally housing small-time merchandise or services; for example: hosiery, photo developing.

lease [LEASING/GENERAL] A contract transferring the right to the possession and enjoyment of property for a definite period of time.

The signed agreement between landlord and tenant that establishes responsibility, sets standards, and states what is recoverable from tenants for the maintenance process.

lease abstract [ACCOUNTING/LEASING/LEGAL] A short version of a lease, containing the most important facts about it in order to facilitate later reviews (for example, by new employees).

lease administration [ACCOUNTING] The function of administering, managing, collecting amounts due and enforcing the provisions in a lease.

lease logs   [LEASING] Logs not only inform team members about the current status of negotiations or a lease agreement prior to the tenant opening for business, but also provide a historical perspective for future use. Logs provide one of the most valuable permanent records of the party's intent from the time negotiations begin until the final agreement is executed. Leasing representatives record the negotiation's essential aspects, whether they were communicated by the tenant or provided by the real estate committee, and whether written or verbal.

lease plan   [LEASING] A detailed plan showing the size and configuration of each space located within the shopping center. Each space is typically numbered for quick identification.

lease summary report   [ACCOUNTING/LEASING] An abstract of information about the status of the leasable space in a center as well as pertinent information from each tenant's lease.

leased space   [LEASING/ACCOUNTING] The measurement used to define how much space a tenant has leased in a center. The leased premise is determined by measuring the distance between the middle walls of a space and the distance between front outside wall to back outside wall.

leasing fees and commissions   [ACCOUNTING/LEASING] The expenses incurred for commissions paid to secure tenants for a center.

leasing representative   [LEASING] A mall employee whose responsibilities include property management, maintaining good relations with tenants, lease administration and negotiation, liaison with ownership, capital improvement and coordination.

leasing summary   [LEASING/ACCOUNTING] A form used by owners and managers to summarize or briefly state the most important lease terms. It is also known as a lease abstract. Typically, some of the information included in the summary or abstract includes the following: tenant trade name; address; space identification and size; use clause summary; percentage rent and breakpoint; rental due date; unusual lease provisions; rent start date; expiration date; escalation dates; tenant legal name and entity; phone/fax numbers; dimensions of the space; minimum rent amount; common area maintainance, tax, utility, marketing fees; late fee amount and application date; security deposit amount; possession date; option dates; and insurance requirements.

lessee   [LEASING/GENERAL] The tenant; one who rents or leases property from another.

lessor   [LEASING/GENERAL] The owner; one who rents or leases property to another.

let   [LEASING] To rent or lease.

letter of intent   [LEASING/LEGAL] Generally a document submitted prior to a formal lease. It serves to delineate the intentions between the landlord and the tenant. Basic issues, including minimum rent, percentage rent, pass-through expenses, and other major points of negotiation, are outlined. Generally subject to execution of a complete contract.

The expression of a desire to enter into a contract without actually doing so.

license agreement   [LEASING/LEGAL] A short-term space rental contract between the licensor (property owner) and the licensee (retailer) that defines the location, term, charges, and responsibilities of each party to the other. Perhaps the most important and defining aspects of the license agreement are that it transforms no estate or interest in the property and is ordinarily revocable at the will of the entity granting the license, and is not assignable. It is intended to not convoke tenancy rights as typically permitted by law in many jurisdictions.

long-term lease [LEASING/GENERAL] A general term that may refer to a lease ten years or longer in term, or, in some areas, five years or longer.

market rent [LEASING/FINANCE] Properly, an amount based on sales potential of various types of retailers that together can do the optimum business in a particular center if it were properly leased by merchandise categories, and as compared to the total occupancy cost each retailer is able to pay and still make a profit. This is other than what is necessary to produce a desired return on investment or to cover development costs; the rate at which space would be leased if offered in a current competitive market based on similar sales and performance; sometimes used interchangeably with *budgeted rent* or *appraisal rent.*

merchandise mix [LEASING] The variety and categories of merchandise offered by the retail tenants assembled in a particular shopping center.

A merchandise mix is a group of products that are closely related because they satisfy a class of needs, are used together, or are sold to the same basic market targets. It is made up of a series of demand-related merchandise items, which are specific versions of a product that has a separate designation.

merchandise plan [LEASING] A forecast, usually by months for a six-month season, of the major elements that enter into gross margin. It normally includes the planning of sales, stocks, purchases, markups, and markdowns.

minimum rent [ACCOUNTING/LEASING/GENERAL] The basic rent a tenant pays; usually expressed as a price per square foot.

Rent that is not based on a tenant's sales.

The specific dollar amount paid by a tenant for the amount of square footage leased.

The basic rent that a tenant will pay the landlord each year, in twelve equal, consecutive installments, computed based on an amount of rent per square foot; also called **base rent.**

mom-and-pop store [LEASING/RETAIL] A store whose owners own only that single store.

natural breakpoint [LEASING/ACCOUNTING] *See* breakpoint.

negotiated inducements [LEASING] Any incentives offered by a landlord to persuade a tenant to commit to a lease. As known factors that will definitely occur, such as tenant improvement construction allowances or free rent periods, these are quantifiable in terms of amount and timing.

net-net lease [LEASING/LEGAL] *See* double net lease.

nonanchors [LEASING] Stores or establishments that do not serve as primary traffic generators (generally, tenants), excluding any freestanding units.

nonretail tenants [LEASING] Shopping center tenants, primarily service-oriented tenants, who do not fit into the traditional category of retailers; a tenant selling services, not goods.

occupancy cost [ACCOUNTING/LEASING/RETAIL] The sum of a tenant's fixed rent, percentage rent, and add-ons. Also called total rent.

outposting [MARKETING/LEASING] The practice of placing a long-term in-line tenant in a cart, kiosk, or temporary in-line location to help the tenant market a new or special product line, for example.

overage rent   [LEASING/ACCOUNTING] An amount of percentage rent beyond the minimum rent that is derived as a percentage of the tenant's sales that exceed an agreed-upon breakpoint.

pad tenant   [LEASING/GENERAL] A tenant, usually freestanding, located on a separate parcel at the front of a shopping center. Also called an *outlot tenant*.

percentage rent   [ACCOUNTING/LEASING/GENERAL] A percentage of the tenant's total annual sales paid in addition to fixed rent. This additional rent is normally paid after a predetermined sales level has been achieved. The percentage factor is then applied to all sales over the present level (breakpoint).

The payment by a tenant as rent of a specified percentage of the gross income from sales made upon the premises. Developers in shopping centers customarily charge a minimum rent plus a percentage rent when sales exceed a certain volume.

Percentage rent is a function of sales activity. A tenant's sales during a lease year are multiplied by the percentage rent rate(s); any excess over the minimum rent is percentage rent.

Extra rent paid to a landlord if a tenant's sales figures exceed a prearranged figure.

permanent tenant   [LEASING] A tenant that has signed a lease with a term longer than one year.

pro rata share   [ACCOUNTING] The assessment of expenses on a proportional basis between landlord and tenant.

pushcart   [LEASING] A movable retail merchandising unit usually located in a center's common area where a merchant sells products and services.

quote rates   [LEASING] Typically expressed in dollars per square foot of a tenant's or prospective tenant's proportionate share of common area maintenance (CAM), real estate taxes and other ongoing shopping center charges based on budgeted expense and budgeted occupancy.

radius restriction   [LEASING/GENERAL] *See* competing business.

rate of retention   [LEASING] The rate at which existing tenants renew their leases in their existing spaces.

remodeling allowance   [LEASING] An allowance offered by the landlord to the tenant to entice the tenant to prepare the leased premises for the tenant's occupancy. It may include a tenant improvement allowance, moving allowance, space plan/drawing allowance, and/or lease buyout. *See* tenant allowance.

rent relief   [LEASING] An abatement of some or all rent in the case of an event that interferes with a tenant's ability to use its space.

rent roll or **rent schedule**   [LEASING/ACCOUNTING] A summary schedule listing of all spaces in a shopping center, vacant as well as occupied, for quick reference and full disclosure. Information listed here includes tenant names by retail category, size of each store, fixed minimum annual rent, the term of each lease (including commencement and expiration dates), the annual percentage rent breakpoint for each tenant and the percentage rent rate(s), as well as other information.

rental area   [LEASING] The square footage of a building that can actually be rented. (Halls, lobbies, elevator shafts, maintenance rooms and lavatories are excluded.)

That part of gross floor area used exclusively by individual tenants and on which rent can be obtained.

retail merchandising unit (RMU)   [LEASING] A state-of-the-art updating of the traditional pushcart, using modern design and materials to create a durable and functional display on which to showcase a specialty tenant's wares or services. The RMU, staffed from the outside like the pushcart, is considerably larger and may be square, rectangular, round, or even elliptical. It is also mobile, although rolling casters mounted underneath have replaced the pushcart's large wagon wheels. Many designs incorporate large display areas, ample storage, high-intensity lighting and modern security features.

RMU   [LEASING] Retail merchandising unit. *See* cart; retail merchandising unit.

short-term lease   [LEASING] *See* long-term lease.

single net lease   [LEASING/RETAIL] A property lease in which the lessee agrees to pay rent plus its proportinate share of the property's real estate taxes. Also called closed-end lease.

specialty leasing program   [LEASING] A program for establishing temporary tenants either in-line or on the common area of a shopping center, also known as *temporary tenant programs.*

specialty license agreement   [LEASING] The signed agreement between a licensor and licensee in which rights, duties, and standards are outlined for application in short-term activities such as carts, kiosks, and retail merchandising unit (RMU) operations. The license agreement is intended to diminish any tenancy rights protected under various jurisdictions.

specialty retail leasing   [LEASING] The process of increasing shopping center net operating income (NOI) and merchandise variety by licensing for a fee, usually for one year or less, space within the shopping center.

sublease   [LEASING/LEGAL] The renting or leasing of premises by a tenant to a third party, but with some portion or interest in them still being retained. Either all or part of the premises may be subleased, for either the whole term of the original lease or a portion of it. However, if the tenant relinquishes his or her entire interest, it is no longer considered a sublease but an assignment.

The original tenant remains liable for the lease while a new tenant assumes occupancy.

temporary occupancy agreement   [LEASING] The signed agreement between a short-term occupant licensee in an in-line space, similar to the specialty license agreement.

temporary tenant   [LEASING] Retailers that lease space for periods of usually less than a year. They are housed in merchandising units such as carts, kiosks, and tall-wall mall stalls, most often located in the shopping center's common areas, vacant in-line spaces, parking lots, and peripheral areas.

temporary tenant program   [LEASING] *See* specialty leasing program.

tenant allowance (TA)   [LEASING/FINANCE] A provision sometimes made by landlords to build a tenant space or provide rent concessions, even free rent, for a period of time to induce the tenant to lease. *See* tenant improvement allowance.

tenant improvement allowances   [LEASING] Provisions in a lease in which the landlord agrees to pay for certain changes to enhance a tenant's space.

tenant improvements [LEASING] Building improvements that enhance a tenant's space. May be paid for by either landlord or tenant and induce the tenant to lease. *See* tenant allowance.

tenant mix [LEASING] The distribution of store types within a retail complex.

The types and price levels of retail and service businesses within a shopping center.

tenant representatives or **tenant reps** [LEASING] Brokers commissioned to handle leasing for and by retail tenants.

triple net lease [ACCOUNTING/LEASING] A lease in which 100 percent of all taxes, insurance, and maintenance associated with a shopping center is paid by the tenant.

turn key [LEASING] The landlord builds and finishes out a retail space; the tenant shows up with merchandise and is ready for business.

unnatural breakpoint [LEASING/ACCOUNTING] A set sales hurdle, negotiated and entered in a lease, that can be used to determine payments by a tenant to the landlord unrelated to the tenant's actual (natural) breakpoint.

use clause [LEASING/LEGAL] A clause inserted into a shopping center retail lease that restricts the category of merchandise or items that a retailer is allowed to sell.

An outline of the exact type of merchandise to be sold or business to be conducted in the premises.

Tenants are restricted to providing the categories of merchandise or services specified in their leases and must obey any lease restrictions on how they operate.

vanilla box [LEASING/CONSTRUCTION] A space partially completed by the landlord based on negotiations between tenant and landlord. Although every landlord's definition is different, a vanilla box normally means HVAC (heating, ventilation and air-conditioning), walls, floors, stockroom wall, basic electrical work, basic plumbing work, rear door and storefront.

warm brick [LEASING] Term for the unfinished space a tenant is given in a shopping center; the tenant is responsible for paying for all costs of store construction.

white box [LEASING] A space partially completed by the landlord or licensor based on negotiations with the tenant, and usually including HVAC (heating, ventilation and air-conditioning) systems, walls, floors, a stockroom wall and door, basic electrical and plumbing work, a rear door and a storefront; also called a vanilla box.

year-end adjustments [LEASING] Adjustments made at year-end addressing the reality of the prior year's operations rather than the estimates. Any adjustments are based on a review of both the general ledger and charges to the common area budgets. Final adjustments must be accurate and presented to tenants in a timely manner.

Index